WHAT NURSERY SCHOOL TEACHERS ASK US ABOUT

EMOTIONS AND BEHAVIOR MONOGRAPHS
Monograph No. 5

edited by
George H. Pollock, M.D., Ph.D.
Chicago Institute for Psychoanalysis

WHAT NURSERY SCHOOL TEACHERS ASK US ABOUT

Psychoanalytic Consultations in Preschools

Editor Erna Furman
Cleveland Center for Research in Child Development,
Cleveland, Ohio

INTERNATIONAL UNIVERSITIES PRESS, INC.

Madison   Connecticut

Library of Congress Cataloging-in-Publication Data

What nursery school teachers ask us about.

    (Emotions and behavior monographs; monograph 5)
    Bibliography: p.
    Includes index.
    1. Mentally ill children—Education (Preschool)—
Ohio—Cleveland. 2. Problem children—Education
(Preschool)—Ohio—Cleveland. 3. Child psychotherapy—
Ohio—Cleveland. I. Furman, Erna. II. Series: Emotions
and behavior monographs; no. 5
LC4182.03W45 1986   371.92′8   86-4346
ISBN 0-8236-6890-4
ISSN 0734-9890
          Manufactured in the United States of America

Contents

Contributors

ERNA FURMAN is a nonmedical child psychoanalyst and licensed psychologist. She is a faculty member of the Cleveland Center for Research in Child Development's Analytic Psychotherapy Training Program of the Cleveland Psychoanalytic Institute and of the Department of Psychiatry, Case Western Reserve University School of Medicine. As a qualified teacher she has taught at all levels and is especially active in applying psychoanalytic findings in the field of education. In addition to treating children and working with parents, she has conducted several of the Center's research projects.

ROBERT A. FURMAN, M.D., is the Director of the Cleveland Center for Research in Child Development and of the Hanna Perkins Therapeutic Nursery School and Kindergarten, in charge of all their many programs and activities. He is also a training analyst in child and adult psychoanalysis at the Cleveland Psychoanalytic Institute, a child psychiatrist on the faculty of Case Western Reserve University School of Medicine, and was a board certified pediatrician. In addition to his ongoing clinical work with patients and teaching commitments, he has served in a number of professional organizations and was recently President of the Association for Child Psychoanalysis.

RUTH HALL is the Director of Therapy at the Hanna Perkins School and a faculty member of the Cleveland Center for Research in Child Development's Training Program in Analytic Psychotherapy. She is a nonmedical child psychoanalyst as well as an experienced speech therapist and specialist in speech pathology. In addition to her psychoanalytic work with children and parents, she utilizes her

professional background in consulting with the United
Cerebral Palsy Association.

MARIA KAISER is a preschool educator with degrees in early
childhood education and in curriculum and instruction and
has extensive classroom experience. She is the Associate
Director of the Society for Crippled Children of Cuyahoga
County, Ohio, and the Director of its Technical Assistance
Project, in charge of placing children with disabilities, and
training staff. Originally a participant in our Center's
courses for teachers, Mrs. Kaiser has for some years been
an active member of our Teacher Training Advisory Committee.

ARTHUR L. ROSENBAUM, M.D., is a psychiatrist, child psychoanalyst, training analyst at the Cleveland Psychoanalytic
Institute, and a faculty member of the Department of Psychiatry, Case Western Reserve University School of Medicine. In addition to his clinical practice and teaching
commitments, he works with parents and children at the
Hanna Perkins School and is a member of its Administra-
tive Committee.

Preface

This book addresses a number of topics which are of perennial concern to educators of nursery school children. Its thinking has evolved from long years of close cooperative endeavor between the teachers at the Hanna Perkins Therapeutic Nursery School and Kindergarten, the child specialists and child psychoanalysts from the Cleveland Center for Research in Child Development, and the families we serve.

Since the early 1950s, we have worked together to study and meet the developmental needs of young children (Furman and Katan, 1969). We accept only youngsters with emotional difficulties in our nursery school and kindergarten, which has 15 children in each group. The parents, especially the mother or primary caretaker, work with a child psychotherapist one hour weekly, trying to unravel the source of their child's troubles with growing up and helping him to master them. The teachers provide a sound educational program, keep in daily touch with the parents, and support their work with the child in many ways; for example, they share detailed observations, alert the child and parents to manifest difficulties, assist all children with recognition and verbalization of feelings and mastery of impulses, and follow up on individual educational and therapeutic measures initiated through the parents' work with the therapist. They also consult weekly with the child psychotherapist who regularly observes in the classroom. Children whose problems cannot be resolved through the teamwork of parents–teachers–therapist, receive additional individ-

ual treatment with the therapist. This close and fruitful
cooperation was early on extended in a modified form to
the day nurseries of the Cleveland Day Nursery Association and adapted to their caretaking and educational
settings, thanks to the initiative and support of Eleanor
Hosley, director of the Day Nursery Association and ad-
ministrator of Hanna Perkins for many years. Regular
consultation meetings between each day nursery and the
assigned child analyst focused on discussion of developmental tasks, educational methods, work with parents,
and concerns about individual children. In addition,
yearly courses on various aspects of child development
provided an opportunity for in-service training and continuing education of the staff. In this way the detailed in-
depth understanding gained in treating a small number
of children at Hanna Perkins could be applied to assist
many more youngsters and their families and utilized for
the prevention of emotional problems.

This work aroused so much interest in the wider community of preschool educators that The Cleveland Association for the Education of Young Children soon asked
our Center to provide similar services for their members—cooperative and private nursery schools, day care
centers, and toddler groups. Since the 1960s we have
worked with many of these skilled and gifted educators
in ongoing consultation groups and courses, a venture
which has proved mutually instructive.

In thus working closely with hundreds of teachers and
child care workers, we found that certain topics were of
special concern, and that discussion frequently focused
on how to understand and handle them. At the teachers'
request, we singled them out, one by one, and made them
the subject of special presentations and annual work-
shops for those who care for young children. Since these
topics are not often dealt with in the literature, or at least

not approached with dynamic understanding, we also put them in writing. Many participants wanted to reread and rethink them at leisure and share them with their colleagues as well as with the parents of their pupils. Some of these articles appeared in educational journals or were distributed as pamphlets through our Center. Publishing them in book form will make them more accessible to interested professionals and parents.

Erna Furman

Acknowledgments

Chapter 1, The Roles of Parents and Teachers in the Life of the Young Child (Erna Furman) was originally presented at "Week of the Young Child," a Meeting of the Cleveland Association for the Education of Young Children, April 1977, Cleveland. It was previously published in *CAEYC Review*, Part I, Fall 1977: 10–15; and Part II, Spring 1978: 12–17.

Chapter 2, The Father–Child Relationship (Robert A. Furman, M.D.) was originally presented at the Annual Workshop for Preschool Educators and Mental Health Professionals, Cleveland Center for Research in Child Development, September 1983, Cleveland. It was previously published in the Pamphlet Series of the Cleveland Center for Research in Child Development, 1983.

Chapter 3, On Separation at Entry to Nursery School (Robert A. Furman, M.D.) was originally presented at the meeting of the Midwestern Association for the Education of Young Children, Annual Conference, April 23, 1966, Cleveland. It was previously published under the title "Experiences in Nursery School Consultations" in *Young Children*, Vol. 22, 1966, 2: 1–12, Washington, D.C.: National Association for the Education of Young Children; and also in Katherine Read Baker, ed. (1972) *Ideas That Work With Young Children*, Washington, D.C.. NAEYC, pp. 225–236. This chapter is reprinted here with the kind permission of the National Association for the Education of Young Children.

Chapter 4, Stress in the Nursery School (Erna Furman) was originally presented at the meeting of the

Cleveland Association for the Education of Young Children, February 1971, Cleveland. It was previously published in *CAEYC Review*, Spring 1982: 23–34.

Chapter 5, Discipline (Erna Furman) was originally presented at the Annual Workshop for Preschool Educators and Mental Health Professionals, Cleveland Center for Research in Child Development, April 1970, Cleveland. It was previously published in the Pamphlet Series of the Cleveland Center for Research in Child Development, 1982.

Chapter 6, Living with Spiderman et al.—Mastering Aggression and Excitement (Ruth Hall) was originally presented at the Meeting of the Cleveland Association for the Education of Young Children, November 19, 1981, Cleveland.

Chapter 7, Learning to Feel Good About Sexual Differences, (Erna Furman) was originally presented at the Annual Workshop for Preschool Educators and Mental Health Professionals, Cleveland Center for Research in Child Development, September 1984. It was previously published in the Pamphlet Series of the Cleveland Center for Research in Child Development, 1984.

Chapter 8, Helping Children with Speech (Ruth Hall) was originally presented at the Annual Workshop for Preschool Educators and Mental Health Professionals, Cleveland Center for Research in Child Development, September 1982. It was previously published under the title "Speech Development—Its Tie to Communication with Mother" in the Pamphlet Series of the Cleveland Center for Research in Child Development, 1982.

Chapter 9, The Child with a "Difference" in the Nursery Group (Robert A. Furman, M.D.) was presented under the title "Further Experiences in Nursery School Consultations" at the Joint Meeting of the Tennessee Association on Children Under Six and the Hamilton County

Mental Health Association, October 27, 1967, Chatta-
nooga, Tennessee.

Chapter 10, Children with Toddlerlike Behavior in
the Nursery School (Erna Furman) was originally presented at the Annual Workshop for Preschool Educators
and Mental Health Professionals, Cleveland Center for
Research in Child Development, October 1980, Cleveland. It was previously published in the Pamphlet Series
of the Cleveland Center for Research in Child Development, Cleveland, 1982.

Chapter 11, Toddlerlike Behavior: Two Case Examples—1 (Arthur L. Rosenbaum, M.D.) was originally presented at the Annual Workshop for Preschool Educators
and Mental Health Professionals, Cleveland Center for
Research in Child Development, October 1980, Cleveland. It was previously published in the Pamphlet Series
of the Cleveland Center for Research in Child Development, Cleveland, 1982.

Chapter 12, Toddlerlike Behavior: Two Case Exam-
ples—2 (Maria Kaiser) was originally presented at the
Annual Workshop for Preschool Educators and Mental
Health Professionals, Cleveland Center for Research in
Child Development, October 1980. It was previously pub-
lished in the Pamphlet Series of the Cleveland Center for
Research in Child Development, Cleveland, 1982.

Chapter 13, Helping Children Cope With Death (Erna
Furman) was originally presented at the Annual Workshop for Preschool Educators and Mental Health Professionals, Cleveland Center for Research in Child
Development, May 1975, Cleveland. It was previously
published in *Young Children*, 33, 1978, 4: 25–32; in Leah
Adams and Betty Garlick, eds. (1979), *Ideas that Work
with Young Children*, Vol. 2, Washington, D.C.: NAEYC,
pp. 186–193; in Janet F. Brown, ed. (1982), *Curriculum
Planning for Young Children*, Washington, D.C.: NAEYC,

1982, pp. 238–245; and in James L. Thomas, ed. (in press), Phoenix, Arizona: The Oryx Press. This chapter is reprinted here with the kind permission of the National Association for the Education of Young Children.

Chapter 14, The Abused Child in the Nursery School (Erna Furman) was originally presented at the Annual Workshop for Preschool Educators and Mental Health Professionals, Cleveland Center for Research in Child Development, October 1981, Cleveland. It was previously published in the Pamphlet Series of the Cleveland Center for Research in Child Development, Cleveland, 1981.

Chapter 15, Readiness for Kindergarten (Erna Furman) was originally presented at the Meeting of the Cleveland Association for the Education of Young Children, February 1976, Cleveland. It was previously published in the *North American Montessori Teachers' Association Quarterly*, 2, 1977, 3: 28–44.

Part I

Chapter 1

The Roles of Parents and Teachers in the Life of the Young Child

Erna Furman

It is barely a generation ago that many considered nursery school unnecessary for a young child as long as he had his parents or parent-substitutes to care for him. It was held that a good mother could teach her youngster all the skills he needed. At present, by contrast, we hear more often that it is unnecessary for parents to care for their underfives as long as a good nursery school or day care center is available. In fact, it is sometimes stated that the school or day care center meets the child's needs more adequately because it provides greater opportunities for intellectual and social growth than are found in the home. Both viewpoints are based on the assumption that, with preschoolers, the roles of parents and teachers are almost identical, that a mother can be a teacher and that a teacher can be a mother. This appears to me to be a misunderstanding of a young child's developmental needs and of the role of the environment in facilitating his maturation. Let us look more closely at what a par-

ent–child relationship and a teacher–pupil relationship
consist of, and let us then turn to discussing some related
questions: When is a young child capable of forming a
teacher–pupil relationship? How can parent and teacher
foster the child's mastery of this developmental step?
What are some of the interferences in cooperation between parent and teacher?

THE PARENT–CHILD RELATIONSHIP

D. W. Winnicott (1940) stated that there is no such
thing as a baby. He meant that a baby is not an independent entity since it would not survive, much less
thrive and prosper, without the consistent round-the-
clock care of a mothering person. Initially she senses and
meets all of the baby's needs and he, in turn, uses her
person and body to gratify all his impulses. In time, and
through this care, the mother enables her baby to become
a person in his own right and she supports his abilities
to recognize and care for his own needs and to modify and
control his urges. Similarly, she at first mediates between
the baby and the outside world, at times shielding him
from it, at other times regulating to what extent and in
what manner he should be exposed to it. And later on she
helps him to deal independently with the world of people
and things. In keeping with his dependence on the mothering person, the child is essentially part of a twosome
throughout baby- and toddlerhood. He forms other relationships as well, but these are either additions to the
mother–child relationship, requiring the mother's presence, or they are substitutes for her during her absence.
An example of the former is a young toddler's relationship
with his older sibling with whom he joyfully engages in
"their" special games within sight or hearing of the
mother. When a need arises, however, the toddler quickly

abandons his sibling and demands mother's comfort. When this same older sibling functions as "sitter," assigned to care for his little brother or sister during mother's absence, the toddler expects him to behave like mother, protests if the sibling-sitter does not approximate mother's care, and treats him as a mother-substitute rather than as a playmate. It is only in the later phase of toddlerhood, usually between the ages of 2 to 3 years, that the child turns to other members of the family as people in their own right, appreciates their different functions, and maintains with them separate relationships which require neither the mother's presence nor her attributes. Father and siblings now acquire a new and important meaning, grandparents are sought, and interest in adults outside the family begins. The mother's role includes recognizing the child's new potential for specific relationships and to provide opportunities for such relationships to materialize. One way in which the parents meet their young child's new need is to choose a nursery school where the child will have a chance to relate to a teacher.

THE TEACHER–PUPIL RELATIONSHIP

In contrast to the early, all-embracing mother–child relationship and in contrast also to the subsequent intimate relationships with the father and other family members, the teacher–pupil relationship is much less intense and much more circumscribed in duration and function. It is a task-oriented relationship whose goal is a common interest—to pursue knowledge, skills, and activities which are not primarily related to personal needs and do not bring direct bodily gratifications. Some of these interests teacher and pupil may share from the start; for example, a youngster may like to draw and paint and may be pleased to find that the teacher too enjoys these activities, is willing to provide appropriate materials, to paint with him, and to help him advance toward more varied or better skills in this area. In many more instances, however, it is the child's relationship with his teacher that paves the way to developing interests and wanting to learn new things. The love for the teacher helps to kindle the interest in what she offers, the pleasure in sharing her activities, the wish to emulate her and to seek her help in this process. The teacher in her turn shows her liking of the child by introducing him to new areas of inquiry and skill, by sharing her enjoyment in them with him, and by supporting and appreciating his participation and increasing mastery. This type of relationship, with its focus on knowledge, skills, and activities, largely excludes caring for the child's bodily needs and gratifying his impulses. Young children can, at best, engage in this kind of relationship for limited periods. After a given period they tire of the necessary effort, the newly acquired pursuits no longer feel pleasurable, bodily needs and urges demand direct satisfaction, and the children long to return to their parent–child relationships. And when they are sick or under stress, children find it altogether impossible to be pupils, and require parents rather than teachers.

In comparing the parent–child relationship with the teacher–pupil relationship, it is at once evident that a child needs to have reached a rather advanced stage in personality development in order to maintain a teacher–pupil relationship, and that this relationship is an addition to, rather than a substitute for the relationship with the parents. We can go a step further and state that a child can only develop a teacher–pupil relationship when he is firmly rooted in his relationship with his parents and when he can use the parent–child relationship as a base from which to venture out, knowing and feeling that it is there to return to at any time.

Can a teacher be a mother as well by including in her job maternal functions such as feeding the child, assisting him with toileting, bathing, and dressing, having him nap in her care, gratifying his need for physical affection by hugging and fondling him? A young child's teacher usually has to fulfill some parental functions when the child cannot look after his needs independently, or cannot yet master his impulses, but even the most caring teacher makes a poor mother. The teacher's time with the child is always limited to her working hours; she is never there at night, on weekends, or holidays; she excludes the child for the most part from her family life; she expects him to share her with a considerable number of other children of the same age and with the same developmental needs, and he never has her all to himself. When the child is sick, she calls in someone else to take him away and requests that he not come back until he is well again. And insofar as she does meet the child's bodily needs, her ministrations are not intimate expressions of her bond with him but are relatively impersonal, prompted by necessity, and largely geared to furthering the child's independence. For example, lunch at nursery school is not cooked by the teacher, no attempt is made to cater to the individual child's special tastes, and the children usually serve themselves and scrape their plates. It is not surprising that when children relate to teachers as if they were mothers, they tend to become very disappointed and frustrated. At the same time, the more a teacher functions as a mother the less does she offer the child an opportunity for establishing a teacher–pupil relationship.

A similar difficulty besets the mother's role as a teacher. In many ways parents are teachers and many mothers are particularly skilled teachers. However, since they maintain a parent–child relationship with their youngster, they cannot help him to relate to them exclusively as a teacher. When a child gets sick in the middle of a mother's "teaching session" with her child she immediately takes care of him as a mother and steps out of her role as teacher. Moreover, the longstanding, intimate parental tie with the child contains many intense feelings and bodily interactions, all part of a complex, deep mutual investment in one another. This cannot be simply set aside at a teaching–learning time, at least not by the child. The relationship with the parent is therefore different from the separate, less intense, time limited, and task oriented relationship to a teacher who does not attempt to be a parent (although she may at times need to perform some functions associated with parental care, such as serving a meal, helping with dressing, putting on a Band-aid, or giving a hug).

Many toddlers and preschoolers attend nursery schools and day care centers before they are developmentally capable of forming a teacher–pupil relationship. Appropriately, they relate to the day care worker or teacher in these settings as mother-substitutes, as sitters. They may master the special stresses inherent in the transition between mothering person and mother-substitute and learn to cope well, but this accomplishment differs from learning to relate to a teacher as a pupil and does not necessarily prepare children for doing so. Many youngsters fail to take this important step in personality growth at a later time, either because they got "stuck" at the earlier level and cannot leave it behind, or because they are not helped enough to appreciate and accomplish the progressive change. Such children continue to view the teacher primarily as a mother-substitute, expect parental gratifications from her, and experience difficulty in utilizing the school and teacher for learning.

HOW CAN A PARENT GAUGE WHEN THE CHILD IS CAPABLE OF FORMING A RELATIONSHIP WITH A TEACHER?

When a child reaches readiness for a teacher–pupil relationship he is master of a number of developmental tasks. In the area of bodily care he has essentially taken on mother's jobs, is independent, and likes to do for himself. He is able to feed himself, using basic implements, he toilets himself, knows when he needs to eliminate, how to wipe himself, and how to wash his hands. He can dress himself at least to the extent of putting on and taking off the simpler clothes and footwear. Above all, he is keen to do for himself and takes pride in accomplishing each new step. He also makes sure that his body is safe: around the house and outside he has learned pretty well how to avoid common dangers (for example, electric plugs, hot stoves and irons, window ledges) and he quickly recognizes when he is hurt and does not feel well. An additional helpful indication of readiness is when the child knows and cares about his belongings, when he recognizes his clothes and toys, takes pride of ownership in them, and looks out for them at least some of the time.

The ability to communicate in words is another prerequisite. It is not so important that the child command a large vocabulary or intricate syntax but rather that he be able to use speech to convey his needs, begin to express his thoughts and feelings in words, and know how to listen to others.

The child's interests and activities provide further signs of readiness. Is he beginning to use toys for fantasy games and role playing (as in "dress up"), and for the acquisition of skills (such as tricycling, ball playing, block building)? Is he interested in activities that do not bring immediate and direct gratification, such as stories, cooking, and crayoning? Does he inquire into things, people, and events for the sake of understanding their purpose or function (e.g., "What does the steamshovel do?"; "Who makes it work?")? Does he pursue a topic with a series of questions and remember the answers? Is he willing to expend some effort in mastering a skill? Does he persist in listening to the end of the story?

A most important area is the child's ability to deal with short-term separations. Does he listen to mother preparing him for her going out, where she will be, for how long, who will be with him? Does he ask questions to further his understanding? Does he verbalize his dislike, or protest against all or some of the plans, but is able nonetheless to accept the situation? Can he behave reasonably well with a familiar sitter and carry on his usual activities? Can he welcome mother back, tell her some of what happened during her absence, and how he felt? Does he ask questions as to what she did while she was away and did he keep in mind what he had been told about it before she left?

Parents often, and I think erroneously, single out "having nice playmates" and "getting along with the other children" as the main purpose of nursery school. Actually the child's wish or need for the companionship of peers is of less import. To start with it suffices if other children are tolerated and if parallel play with them seems pleasurable.

Usually children accomplish these developmental steps around 3 or 3½ years and are then ready for nursery school or, more specifically, ready to take the big developmental step of forming a relationship with a teacher.

HOW DOES A TEACHER KNOW WHEN A CHILD HAS ESTABLISHED AN APPROPRIATE RELATIONSHIP WITH HER?

Among the many signs of a teacher–pupil relationship the following are readily observed: The child seeks to impress the teacher with everything about himself—size, strength, clothes, possessions, but above all with his performance of skills and achievements at learning tasks ("Look at my picture!"; "See how high I can climb!"). His wish to be admired is paralleled by his admiration for what the teacher has and does. He wants to use her materials, engage in her activities, and acquire her skills ("Let *me* play the xylophone!"; "*I* want to put on the Scotch tape!"). He shares appropriate things and stories from home. He brings stones he found on a walk rather than his teddy bear, and he is more likely to tell of a shopping trip with mother rather than about his struggle over not wanting to go to bed. He knows, accepts and even enjoys the school rules and traditions (sitting in a circle for stories, celebrating another child's birthday at snack time, using small toilets in the bathroom). Rarely does he expect the teacher to perform parental tasks or complain that school is not like home. He does not engage the teacher in body care or demand bodily love from her, so their communication is mainly verbal. He does not expect to monopolize the teacher's time, even though he makes a bid for her positive attention, and he tolerates her care of others. He is ready to leave mother in the morning and welcomes her back at going home time, and he does not tease her by displaying his preference for his teacher and for the school's way of doing things. But he tends to behave better at school than at home. Mothers, and even teachers, sometimes think that this is due to the teacher's better handling of the child. Actually it is in the nature of the closer and deeper parent–child relationship that it inevitably gives rise to more conflicts as well as encompassing many more daily hours. The child's appropriate behavior with his teacher, far from being a discredit to his mother, can be taken as a proof of her good parenting. Without a solid base in the parent–child relationship and without much successful maturation in its framework, a child cannot relate well to a teacher or utilize her teaching efforts.

HOW CAN PARENTS AND TEACHERS FOSTER THE DEVELOPMENT OF A TEACHER–PUPIL RELATIONSHIP?

There is a vast difference between a child's maturational potential for relating to a teacher and his ability to achieve such a relationship. Like all developmental tasks, this one too is slow and difficult, requires much assistance from those who make up the child's environment, and often is not accomplished till the latter part of the nursery school year. Initially, the child usually does not appreciate the difference between a teacher and a mother-substitute, and it is therefore particularly important that the adults not be confused as to their respective roles so that they can assist the child in making the necessary distinction. One little girl struggled for a long time with this concept and, in spite of much help, seemed unable to come to terms with her conflict of loyalties and her difficulty in viewing the teacher as an appropriate additional person in her life. After many months she indicated her mastery when she stated to her mother with great relief, "Now I like you and I like Miss S. It's like when you started to give Jennifer (her baby sister) applesauce. It was not instead of getting milk, she just needed both."

When both parent and teacher recognize how difficult it is for a young child to master the new task, they can empathize with his feeling in words as well as support his efforts in deeds. Already, prior to the start of school, the parent can help by giving preparatory explanations, visiting the school, clarifying the child's misconceptions, and acknowledging his positive and negative feelings about the anticipated experience. Knowing that the child needs the assurance of the continuing relationship with the mother in order to leave her and to build an additional relationship, mother and teacher plan on a very gradual physical separation and assist the child in being aware that there will be no mental separation from mother; that is, her love and concern for him continue throughout her absence. In practice this is helped when the child is brought to school and picked up by the parent so that there is a direct bridge from home to school and back again, and when these parent–teacher contacts are further utilized to exchange relevant daily information; for example, by the parent letting the teacher know of special home events and the teacher reporting to the parent on the child's activities and experiences during his school day. Parents can make a point of telling the child where they will be, what they will do, that they will think of him, and will look forward to learning about his day. The teacher can support this by talking with the child at appropriate times about his parents' whereabouts, about their love for him, and his for them. She can empathize with his mixed feelings when he misses them and can plan with him what he could tell or show them at going home time.

It usually takes about two months for the child to master his initial adjustment, and we take it for granted that these weeks are accompanied by manifestations of his stress and struggle either at home or in school, or in both places (E. Furman, 1969a). We may see behavioral difficulties, expressions of upset feelings, regressions in functioning, and excessive use of self-gratifying habits such as thumbsucking. It is sometimes thought that a smooth, immediate adaptation to nursery school is proof of good handling by parent and teacher. In most instances it is an indication that the child is not really grappling with the task, is not mastering it appropriately, and will run into difficulty at a much later point when the connection with entry to school is no longer readily discernible.

During the entry period as well as later, teachers help to build a teacher–pupil relationship by engaging the child's interest in learning activities and by showing their love for the child in this area—appreciating his efforts and accomplishments, offering him knowledge and materials, sharing with him their enthusiasm for learning and for pursuing activities, and welcoming his contributions. By contrast, the teacher deals with the child's bodily needs and wishes primarily by assisting him in taking care of them himself, by involving herself as little as possible in bodily ministrations and gratifications, and by helping him to direct his intimate emotional concerns to the parent whose domain they are. Among these are the child's bodily interests, his feelings about the members of his family and about home events. For example, when a child complains that mother is angry because he bothers the baby, the teacher may hear him out, sympathize with his troubled feelings, and suggest that he talk it over with mommy. When a child shows confusion over sexual matters or asks questions about them, the teacher may answer briefly, or point out that he seems to be mixed up about this, and then suggest that they will tell mommy about it together at going home time because mommy is the best person to help him with these concerns.

Sometimes the teacher may offer the parents an interview to assist them in working out the difficulty with their child. It usually is not helpful, however, when the teacher takes over their function. If she does so without their permission, parents tend to resent it, and the child may experience a loyalty conflict. If the teacher does take over because the parent does not know how to talk with his child about certain things, the child is tempted to regard the teacher as a parent, to bring all his conflicts into the school setting, and to jeopardize his relationship with his parents as well as the essential relative neutrality of his learning milieu.

Similarly, parents can assist the child by making sure that they deal with the child's needs and urges as much as possible at home and help him with the stresses and puzzlements engendered by home experiences and emotional concerns. They inform the teacher about relevant matters which affect the child so that the child can share them at school if he wishes, and so that the teacher can empathize with the child's feelings and support the parents' work with him. On the other hand, they refer the child to the teacher with those things which specifically belong to school; things he can bring to school to show or share, information he can gather there, or activities he can learn and practice at school. They welcome his accounts of what he has learned, appreciate the pictures he made, admire the new materials he has used. They give explicit permission for their child to follow the school's different rules and traditions and sanction his enjoyment of the different setting.

In this way parents and teachers show respect for and trust in each other's roles with the child, convey harmony in their interaction, build a cooperative relationship with one another, and help the child integrate into his life a teacher–pupil relationship along with his family ties.

There are many ways in which a child can profit from nursery school attendance. Perhaps the most important one is the opportunity to get to know how to learn from and with a teacher. This is crucial to all his subsequent learning and will stand him in good stead when he enters elementary school.

SOME INTERFERENCES IN THE COOPERATION BETWEEN PARENTS AND TEACHERS

Unfortunately, for internal and external reasons, many youngsters fail to master this important developmental task. Among the former are a child's lack of developmental readiness for nursery school, his emotional difficulties at the time of entry, or during his years of attendance, or his reactions to stressful events (illness, bereavement), which take up his mental energies and jeopardize his coping with the nursery school experience. External reasons include inappropriate nursery school settings, unhelpful educational methods at home and at school, and, all too frequently, inadequate adult assistance to the child in his task of forming a teacher–pupil relationship. This is sometimes caused by a misunderstanding or ignorance of the child's needs and is usually compounded by unspoken tensions between parents and teachers.

The child's entry into nursery school represents a new stage in his life, and for the mother especially, a new stage in his relationship with her. She loses the intimate bodily bond with her toddler. The child's maturation necessitates a change from relating through body care and nonverbal communication to a new relationship based on talking to each other and sharing activities with diminishing bodily closeness and emotional exclusiveness. We know separation is frustrating and painful for the youngster who forges ahead. We tend to forget that it is in many ways even harder for the mother who is left behind. She finds it especially stressful when she mistakes the teacher for an additional mother who will absorb some of her child's love and who may handle him better because of her educational expertise and multitude of materials and activities. Most mothers also feel that, in starting nursery school, they expose the products of their mothering to the "expert's" critical eye. If the child experiences difficulties, they, the mothers, will be judged and blamed. Mothering is a very personal business and as mothers we are especially vulnerable to hurt, shame, and guilt whenever our children have troubles or do not seem to reflect well on us. The younger the child, the more this tends to hold true.

It is therefore not surprising that mothers sometimes wish to foreshorten the gradual separation period (it is easier to leave than to be left); that they put a premium on their children's immediate and perfect adjustment to the nursery (fearing that any behavioral difficulty or unhappy feelings betray a failure in mothering); that they tend to avoid hearing much about the child from the teacher (the less you know the better off you are and perhaps the trouble will go away if you put off talking about it); and that they may react defensively when approached by the teacher, either denying the child's difficulties or blaming them on the school (offense is the best defense).

Teachers too feel insecure, especially vis-à-vis parents. It is a trying task to care for a whole group of strange children. One can feel at a real loss when one is unable to comfort one crying 3 year old, prevent another one from hitting his peers, or persuade a third to remain with the group during story time. Whereas many people think that it is easy to make little kids behave, we teachers know that nobody is quite as uncooperative and uncontrollable as a youngster can be, and nobody else can as quickly reduce a teacher's professional self-confidence. In the face of such helplessness and hurt it is easy to per-

suade oneself that the child's obstreperousness is not due
to our lack of educational know-how, our inadequate understanding of his inner stress, or to his lack of trust in
a new person, but is simply caused by his mother ("If she
had brought him up properly . . ."). This tendency to
blame the home rather than oneself leads to a critical or
unduly probing approach to the mother. It is not uncommon for a teacher to link the child's school behavior directly to home events or methods of handling and to give
the mother unsolicited advice on how she could improve
her parenting.

When parent and teacher are preoccupied with warding off their hurt, disappointment, frustration, and fear
of criticism, unhelpful mutual attitudes develop. Differences in methods and rules are not explored, acknowledged, and tolerated but glibly judged good or bad. The
child's difficulties are not approached as puzzles to be
understood and worked out but are blamed on one another; conferences are not welcomed as a means of ex-
changing information and cooperative effort but are
dreaded, postponed, and avoided or lead to a hostile im-
passe. The parent–teacher relationship fails to develop
and the child is the main loser. Instead of getting assistance from the adults, he has to contend with their open
or implicit hostility and competition. He notices his
mother's disapproval of his paint-stained hands (it implies that mother does not go along with the teacher's use

of materials or attitudes toward cleanliness), and he similarly picks up his teacher's glance when mother helps
him with his boots (it implies that teacher does not go
along with mother's ways of showing love through body
care).

When mothers and teachers appreciate their true
roles in the life of the young child, when they can recognize their own feelings of inadequacy, and empathize with

each other's hardships, they can realize that they need one another in order to understand the child, and can work together on the joint task of assisting the child in his development. The teacher needs the mother's help in order to develop a relationship with the child and to understand his personality. The mother needs the teacher's observations in order to learn how her child functions when he is not with her. Both have to learn from and with the child about his concerns, and plan cooperative means of helping him.

For example, a teacher may say, "I badly need your help to understand Jimmy. He has found it difficult to settle down to activities. I don't know why that is. I don't know whether I am not helping him in the right way or whether something in the school bothers him. I don't even know whether he shows this behavior only at school or whether you have observed it at other times and have perhaps found ways of helping him." The mother may have a clue to Jimmy's behavior from what he has told her about school or from how he behaves with her at home. She may have had success or failure in helping him. In either case, she and the teacher can begin to discuss the matter, figure out ways of approaching Jimmy, and of getting to know his ideas and feelings. A joint effort, rather than a mutual reproach, is under way.

A parent–teacher relationship based on respect and focused on common interest in the child's welfare can be established during the trying initial months of nursery school attendance. It will form the framework for later cooperative efforts when the child deals with other stresses which either maturation or accidents of life put in his path.

Chapter 2

The Father–Child Relationship

Robert A. Furman, M.D.

The father–child relationship is an enormous topic. When I tried to consider all its aspects, I found myself saying less and less about more and more. Therefore, I decided to focus selectively on those areas where our research at the Center and Hanna Perkins School has had something to contribute. Our findings do seem to touch on a number of consecutive developmental phases in a way that may provide a coherent view, though not a complete one.

In describing the father's role I will have in mind the average, devoted father who has entered the developmental phase of parenthood. Not all fathers, just as not all mothers, are successful in achieving this goal, but this need not deter us from delineating this role to which we hope all fathers aspire and which many reach as they mature. I shall start with some observations of Winnicott's, both because of their importance as well as because they lead to some thoughts Erna Furman has reported. I will be leaning on aspects of her work in what I will be discussing here.

THE FATHER'S ROLE IN HELPING HIS WIFE TO MOTHER

Winnicott (1964) says that with her newborn the mother should behave in a way which at other times in her life we would have to consider as quite pathological. She should withdraw her investment from the reality world around her to invest herself primarily in the unit that is she and her baby. In this exclusive investment she will accommodate to the transition from the baby within as a part of herself to the baby without, still essentially a part of herself. She will use this unique closeness to get to know her own baby's particular cries and signals, what makes the baby comfortable and uncomfortable, to provide the closeness and responses out of which the baby will learn to recognize her as the one who fulfills its needs and will begin to experience her as the source of pleasure.

Winnicott defines clearly his view of the father's role at this phase of life, a role which in many ways is never to change; modify, yes, but perhaps never to disappear. It is the role of the protector of the mother–child unit and relationship, as if he were to encompass them in his arms and keep them safe from outside interferences so that the mother can devote herself to establishing her relationship with the baby.

This primacy of the mother with the child is something some men, perhaps particularly men who work professionally with children, may have difficulty appreciating emotionally. We all know it intellectually, but I have worked with mothers, wives of professionals, who have felt that their husbands acted as if they knew better and subtly, oh so subtly, have undermined the primacy of the mother's role as caretaker. I was no exception, but was helped very much with this by our pediatrician whom I called when our first baby was first ill. He was an old and dear close friend of mine and so I elected to do the phoning as a kind of comrade-in-arms. His first words to me, when I paused long enough for him to say anything, were, "Please get off the phone and let me talk to the baby's mother."

The view of the father's initial role of protecting and supporting the primacy of the mother–child relationship may say something about my suspicions and reserve about those who see the father's early role as that of a mother substitute. If that is what the mother wants and needs at some moments to get some respite so that she can better return to her tasks as need fulfiller, all fine and good. That would make him a mother substitute at her wish, at her beck and call, in response to her needs, not in response to the father's needs and wishes. Some fathers may need to start their relationship with their child through feeding, diapering, doing some of mother's tasks, and that is all right too, as long as it does not interfere with the mother's mothering. What I am addressing here primarily is how a father deals with his maternal side. All fathers have such a side, not just professionals who work with children. One hopes that, early on in his parenting a father will learn to gratify this part of himself vicariously, through his pride in, support, and protection of his wife's maternal role. In doing so he is of enormous help to the mother and to his child.

In addition to the first months of life, there are two other specific times when the father's relationship to the mother may be crucial for the child's well-being: in the toddler phase and at all those times which Erna Furman (1982) has described when a mother has to be there to be left. During the toddler phase, perhaps more than at any other time—though not exclusively then—a mother's adult personality makeup gets a severe test when she spends hour after hour, day after day, week after week with dirty diapers and bottoms, runny noses, food all over the floor, face, and clothes. It is difficult to confront constantly these early instinctual manifestations, and every woman will need an opportunity to have very civilized, very adult times with her husband to recement her adult personality. We often say that the best thing we could do for our nursery school teachers at Hanna Perkins would be to offer them a candlelight dinner each Friday night, complete with tablecloth, china, crystal, and wine. It need not be such, but I hope the point is clear that the mother of a toddler periodically needs special civilized adult times, be they just simple times of adult conversation.

As to the times of being there to be left, some of these impinge primarily on the mother, for example, weaning and the start of nursery school. At those times a husband who understands and is still there for the mother after she has been left by the child, can be a big help. At later times, start of college, living away from home, marriage of the children, the being left is still hard but it is more readily understood because it affects both parents more equally. It is shared and they can help one another.

THE FATHER'S ROLE IN LOVING HIS CHILD

I would like at this point to move to some of our experiences with children in single-parent homes whom we have gotten to know at Hanna Perkins. The observation was first made in *A Child's Parent Dies* (E. Furman, 1974) that the loss of a parent denies to a child a source of love as well as a person to love. This deprivation is especially serious for children who lost a parent in their first two or three years. Even when these children received the best of early help, it has been impressive to note the unfortunate aftermath of their having sorely missed the extra love from the absent parent. This is not always the case, but it is a frequent enough occurrence, well-enough studied, to allow us to draw some fair inferences about the role a father's loving of his child plays in his child's development.

We have particularly observed the combination of lowered self-esteem, difficulty in mastering aggression, and difficulty in integrating a helpful conscience. Although each of these is a most complex issue, deriving from many sources, it is possible to see and perhaps understand how these three problems relate to one another. The lowered self-esteem perhaps manifests itself earliest. We see it in a lack of adequate pleasure in accomplishments and in a tendency to having one's feelings hurt too easily. The difficulty in mastering aggression shows next, in the exaggerated anger that flares up in response to each of what might otherwise be minor hurts to the feelings. Then, as latency starts and a conscience begins to get integrated into the personality, we note a great deal more of the externalizations that Erna Furman (1980) has described as appropriate to this age. All children experience some difficulty in learning to listen to the "inner voice" of the new conscience which tends to set higher standards than they can meet. Young schoolchildren often avoid this unfamiliar, painful inner conflict by attributing the demands of conscience and its punitive role to the outside world, to the principal who is seen as an ogre, or to the parents who are perceived as excessively strict. With the single-parent child, however, these developmental manifestations are greatly exaggerated and not easily outgrown. There is an increased need to provoke, to get punishment from without, because the child unconsciously prefers it to the threats, reproaches, and punishments meted out by his own conscience which is much too harsh.

We hypothesize that the lowered self-esteem comes from inadequate supplies of love, from missing out on that extra source of love from without that may be available with two parents present. A deficiency of that love inside, a love that should be self-protecting, may mean a deficiency of the love that can tame the aggression all must so struggle to master. If there is enough love it helps the toddler to fuse anger, to modulate and tone down its harsh destructiveness for the sake of loving. Likewise, it helps the preschooler to neutralize his aggression, to transform its energy into zest, and to invest it in activities which will serve constructive ends. When there is not enough inside love, we find that these important steps in personality development are impeded. We also feel that when this anger, which has remained too harsh and too unmodified, later fuels the developing conscience, it accounts for part of the child's trouble with integrating such a conscience and learning to live with it.

If we understand our experiences correctly and if our hypotheses are valid, it is clear that the loving of his children that a father does, contributes to a child's self-esteem, contributes to his mastery of aggression, and contributes to healthy conscience formation. These contributions, often so silently made, seem so significant that I wanted to mention them explicitly. It is true that some children with one parent escape these difficulties, but the risk of problems arising in these areas is much greater without a father's healthy contribution.

How can the mother help her child if a father is not available in the home? It is important to realize that a mother cannot be both a mother and a father, that there will be a void in the fatherless family. The child will know and feel this. The mother cannot fill this void, but if she can acknowledge it with her child and sympathize with his feelings about it, she can preclude the development of a gulf between them which could interfere with what she has to give as a mother.

This brings us to another area of our research that has applicability to our topic. I shall start with an observation from one of the classes in the high school that took our course in child development (E. Furman, 1981). The question always arises whether, in a single-parent family, say with the father absent, his role cannot be fulfilled by an uncle, a grandfather, a friend of the mother? I was interested in the discussion of this question by the high school students. With surprising ease and unanimity, but not without careful deliberation and discussion, one group summed it up rather well by saying unless the man was the child's father, married to the child's mother, he was just different, it just was not the same. They all agreed that something is better than nothing, but that did not change their feeling that for the healthiest and happiest resolution of early childhood there should be a family unit that should consist of mother, father, and child.

What these students were addressing is that crucial period of life that marks the transition from a preschool to a school-aged child, the period of life marked by what psychoanalysts call the resolution of the oedipal phase. It is difficult to discuss our research about this crucial period without becoming either too theoretical or else simplifying the essence out of our thinking. I hope you will bear with me as I try to skirt between these twin dangers.

Preschool teachers know well the struggles of their charges to keep instinctual feelings and thoughts out of their learning and that when children have made the transition to becoming schoolchildren, their sexual wishes and strivings have become more quiescent or latent—hence our designation of the school-aged period as latency. One

second grader in analytic treatment described this well
for me when he said that he knew one day he would like
girls as his teenaged brother now did, but for him this
was hard to believe, as right now girls seemed so "yucky."
The teachers know also that a great repression or forgetting of the earlier years ensues during this transition
time and that the teachers and the preschool experiences
apparently are almost totally forgotten by most school-
aged boys and girls. Preschool teachers also know that
conscience formation is something that ensues from the
struggles that mark this transitional period. For example, kindergarten teachers cannot leave a class alone for
a moment at the start of the year but they can at the end
of the year have some children who can manage on their
own to stay in control for brief periods. These children
have become schoolchildren, latency children with consciences that can function adequately, if the demands are
not too great.

These are the observable phenomena of this transition
period, well known to the observant educator of children
of this age: the instinctual wishes become latent; a repression sets in; and a functioning conscience now appears.
How all this comes about is perhaps not so easy to describe
and we still struggle to understand all that goes into this
transition, what motivates it and sustains it. It would
appear as if the preschooler follows the dictum, "If you
can't lick 'em, join 'em." For the little boy this would
mean surrendering his competition with his father, giving up his instinctual wishes for his mother, modeling
himself on his father. All this somehow ends up with the
boy taking into his personality an image of his father
that becomes the focal point for his developing conscience.

What we have tried to understand is how some boys
and girls come through this transitional period sure of
and content with their sexual identity and are kind, car-

ing, considerate, and giving people with reasonable consciences, while others come through as if chronically discontented with themselves and as rather nasty and selfish human beings with great troubles with their consciences. We believe that fathers have a great deal to do with how this transition period is concluded regarding these vital characterological features.

When a father fulfills the "average, expectable" role with his son, one of kindness, pride, and respect, he becomes a man who cannot be wished ill without great internal stress and pain. A most difficult conflict arises, an unresolvable one unless a boy decides to bow to his love of his father and to the reality of the impossibility of his wishes for his mother. As the oedipal father goes inside somehow to become a boy's conscience, it is more a loving father that is then taken in and a conscience is formed that has a better chance of becoming a helpful aid for growth and development, not just a punitive force and voice. This inside father also becomes a source of identification with the father, acquiring in this way his kind and affectionate and protective aspects. To the extent that reality plays its role in the boy surrendering his wishes, there is less loss of self-esteem, less sense of being the vanquished in a vital struggle. All the prior years of the father's caring availability pay off for the son when he can master this transitional phase with a healthy identification with his father and thus acquire those attributes of kindness, giving, and caring for another.

With his daughter I will want to emphasize a father's ability to give and to be given to. The ultimate in a little girl's wishes for her father in the transitional period revolves around giving and receiving, the wishes to receive and in turn give a baby to the father being the unconscious core. It is easy to see how a father who enjoys his daughters, enjoys their femininity, enjoys supporting it with the gifts he gives them, is a great help to a little girl. He makes their femaleness something prized and respected. He helps further as he can accept their gifts to him, as he can admire and enjoy their efforts at doing the jobs that mother has taught them. Their more instinctual wishes will, of course, be there in full force, but as these are met with affection and not excitement, so he facilitates the mastery of their instinctual base.

THE FATHER'S ROLE IN HELPING CHILDREN DEVELOP SENSIBLE VALUES AND ATTITUDES

In focusing next on the father's relationship with his school-aged children, his children from 6 until puberty, it is possible to understand his role in helping them with their growing up tasks without having to distinguish between his relationships with his sons and daughters.

First comes to view the school-aged child's job of integrating into his or her personality the new conscience and new character attributes, the outcomes of the transition from being a preschool child to being a true school-aged child. These new aspects of the child seem a bit strange and foreign to him at first, the conscience almost sounding like the voice of someone else telling him what is right and wrong, how not to do the wrong. It takes a while before the conscience is truly his and assists him by having him know when something is wrong. Then there is just no issue about doing or not doing it: since it is wrong, it won't be done. It takes a while also before this conscience is not only fully integrated as the child's own, but has become so solidified as a part of him that it will be immune to almost any stresses or temptations, that is, until it has achieved full autonomy.

Until these maturations have taken place, the conscience will seem like a bit of a foreign body but as such will be available for modification. The initial conscience is a bit crude and harsh, always I feel, like a caricature of the parents when angry as seen by a very little child. As latency unfolds, the child will see that when his parents get angry, they are not angry at him in the way his conscience is, and with the help of these experiences the harsh voice of the conscience will change, will come to be more in conformity with the gentler real voice of the parents.

In similar fashion a child can get to see that his earlier impression of the father as only intermittently kind might have been incorrect, and the reality of the father's actual consistently available kindness can buttress identification with this aspect of him. As Erna Furman pointed out in her paper on latency development (1980), some fathers can even discuss with their children aspects of their behavior that they hope the children will not have to copy. The father who is realistically and consistently available does much by his simple presence to enable the child to mature and integrate both conscience and personality attributes.

School is another major developmental task for the child of this period and here again, father can be of great assistance. By his interest and attitude to school and schoolwork, he tells his children so much of his attitude to work, of his aspirations and hopes for them. Not only can his attitude assuage the children's apprehensions about competition with their father, he also supports the maturation of the character attributes of perseverance and responsibility.

All through this period there is also something so important about a father's protection of his children, both sons and daughters. By protection I do not necessarily mean just protection when they are ill, keeping them safe from danger, but would want to include protection from demands that are too much, not age-appropriate, as well as from demands that are not strong enough. Age-appropriate expectations are easy to request, so hard to assess at any particular point in life. But such things as allowance management, job management, and responsibilities at home can often most helpfully be a part of the father's relationship with his school-aged children. How he does his jobs around the house certainly sets an example for them, but equally important, he can make sure they have age-appropriate expectations before them, ones he supports and assists. I used to think only of fathers whose expectations exceeded what was appropriate for a school-aged child. Lately I have been so surprised to see fathers who had too little expectations of their children, in this way subtly telling them not to compete with him or implying that their efforts were not worth being expended.

In addition to supporting the new steps in personality maturation, supporting school and work, the father keeps his long-standing role in introducing the aspects of the outside world that particularly appeal to and interest him. He has the chance to share his own special interests, enriching interests, and share them in a way that can show his children how to play and enjoy, as well as how to work and enjoy. Mother, of course, shows both of these at home herself, but how much more meaningful it is when this example is repeated by father as well.

I worry a bit that what I have said about the father's relationship with his school-aged children might sound too much like his being a model during this period. I worry because I hear so much about "role modeling" that sounds so superficial, almost like acting in certain ways at certain times for the benefit of the children. Rather, what I am trying to point out is the flexibility of the healthy school-aged child's personality that enables it to be modified with the help of the actual reality of what father is as a person. It matters what he is as a person, what his values are, and it matters very much through all this period when the foundation is being completed to start adolescent development. It matters particularly in providing a sensible reality which contrasts with and counteracts the child's unrealistic fantasies, born of his wishes and urges.

THE FATHER WITH HIS ADOLESCENTS

In adolescence what I often call the "due bills" are called in. The time for some personality modification has passed—that was in latency with the school-aged child—and I hope this point will emphasize in retrospect what I said about a father's relationship with his school-aged children. Modification in latency does, of course, have its limitations, as we are all so aware. I hope that emphasizes, in turn, the importance of the father's relationship with his prelatency, preschool children.

I am not implying that what a father does with his adolescent children is of no moment, as such is not the case. Because the adolescent does have lapses with his or her control, because the adolescent sometimes even has to have lapses with control to see what that is all about, a father's consistency with *his* control becomes all the more important. I know of one father who jokingly told his adolescent daughter that, "In our family there is no generation gap." He received the sharp rejoinder, "Oh yes, there is, and don't you forget it." Unruffled, persistent consistency—steadfastness—is what the adolescent boy or girl asks of father. It is a tall order, one they cannot ask of themselves, but it is precisely because they cannot ask it of themselves that they so wish to find it in both their parents.

HOW DOES ONE BECOME A GOOD FATHER?

In concluding this whirlwind tour of the father–child relationship from birth through adolescence, a few words, even if brief ones, seem in order about what may enable a man to father well. I believe a father learns to parent, to put another ahead of self, primarily from his mother; he learns how to father from his own father. He will succeed in his own fathering endeavors as he is able to integrate these two within himself, aided by the marital relationship within which his fathering develops and unfolds.

By way of summary, let me recall that this was no attempt to be inclusive with the very vast topic of the father–child relationship. Instead, after starting with some of Winnicott's thinking, I have tried to focus on the research contributions of our Center and Hanna Perkins School. What I am struck with as I think back about the material, is how much our efforts have been centered on elucidating the method of action of something so easily taken for granted—the quiet, loving role of the good-enough father; his protection of the mother–child couplet, the role his loving plays in promoting mastery of aggression, successful conscience integration, development of adequate self-esteem, mastery of the oedipal phase, passage into schoolchild status with the acquisition of many character traits we so admire and cherish. We all know of the father's traditional roles of protecting and loving. I think what I have been doing is to describe the mechanisms by which these roles are fulfilled and how they facilitate a child's emotional growth and maturation.

Chapter 3

On Separation at Entry to Nursery School

Robert A. Furman, M.D.

We all know that a young child's entry to nursery school is a difficult developmental task. Only continuous observation in the preschool setting can teach us how children grapple with it in different ways and how we can best assist them in this process. No two children are quite alike, but understanding gained with one can throw light on the meaning of the behavior of others. Accordingly, I will discuss the story of just one child and the insights he made available to us. As his teachers, and I as their psychoanalytic consultant, came to understand the problems this boy faced in making the transition from home to school, we could help him master them.

Some years ago I was asked in a special consultation to help with Jimmy who was then about 3½ years old and had been in his school about three months. Jimmy's school teachers believed in trying to make the transition into school a gradual and tolerable one and on the first day had encouraged his mother to stay in the classroom the entire time. Jimmy had stayed by her side staring rather blankly about. The next two days the mother separated easily from Jimmy and waited in an adjoining office where she was available to him, had he wanted her.

Jimmy met his teachers each morning and rather docilely went with them to begin whatever activity had been prepared to start the day. He socialized little with the other children, played by himself with the blocks at free time, ate but part of his juice and crackers at snack time, and left easily with his mother at the end of the morning. He did not avail himself of the opportunity to visit her during the morning.

The pattern had not seemed strange to his teachers who felt he was being perhaps just a bit slow in settling in. They sought a consultation a few months later, however, when this pattern remained essentially unchanged. They specifically asked me about his not talking at school, saying that he only answered the teachers when asked something by them, and answered them only in monosyllables. At home the mother had noticed no change in his activities or behavior. He continued what had correctly seemed to her as age-appropriate speech, although she noted he commented little if at all about his new school. He now came to school with two other children whose mothers alternated with the driving.

The teachers rather wisely and simply made the observation, as they described Jimmy to me, that he managed in a way as if he really wasn't even at school, existing there in a cloud that blocked his contact with teachers and children.

I have selected Jimmy's case because it presents the most common problem that I meet in consultations with preschool groups: separation. Jimmy's teachers were at first a bit surprised that I picked out his trouble as one involving separation. One of his teachers was a bit inexperienced and remarked at once how easily he had separated from his mother and what a nice and gradual indoctrination he had enjoyed in starting school. I had only to point, however, to the teachers' astute observation that he behaved as if he weren't even in school, to underline the simple point that, although his body came willingly to school each day, his heart, mind, and feelings did not. His heart, mind, and feelings still remained out of school at home with his mother and had in reality not separated from her at all.

TWO VITAL DISTINCTIONS

This gave us the opportunity to discuss some very vital distinctions: that there is all the difference in the world between achieving a physical separateness of a child from his home and mother, such as had occurred with Jimmy, and achieving and mastering a true separation—something Jimmy had not yet approached. The second, vital distinction we talked about was between a school's supplying the milieu in which a mother and child might best approach separation, and the actual reality of a mother and child utilizing this opportunity to achieve a mastery of the separation experience.

Jimmy's school had come a long way in a short number of years. They had completely revamped their admission procedures during this period and now would not accept a child unless the mother came with him for his first three sessions, staying in the room for the entire first one. They had stopped supplying any but emergency transportation for 3-year-olds, and had insisted that regardless of whatever transportation a mother worked out she had to bring and fetch him at least two days each week. They always suggested that each mother, if at all possible, do all the driving for her child.

They had evolved this policy after long deliberations when they found that their educational goals were too often unattainable with children who were deposited with them as a kind of baby-sitting service, brought to school and returned home each day from the very first day by school transportation. Once assured of supportive consultation, they felt that they would try including education about separation among their other educational goals. And as they had helped some mothers learn about sublimations, about games and activities appropriate and helpful for the preschooler, so they now also tried to help these mothers see and understand the significance of separation, the need for preparation, for talking about feelings, and for gradually presenting any major change for a child.

With Jimmy, however, it had become clear that despite everyone's best intentions and sound arrangements, he and his mother had not been able to utilize the opportunity the school had offered him. He had slipped past this introductory period by achieving only physical presence in school with no separation accomplished at all.

The situation was not so difficult to approach because Jimmy's mother was most conscientious and interested and the senior teacher felt the mother could help in coping with the problem. She planned on having the mother visit to observe so that she, too, could see and feel Jimmy's lack of presence in school. The mother saw and did understand the situation and changed at once to supplying all of Jimmy's transportation. During these trips she began talking to Jimmy, telling him of her surprise that he reported so little of school to her, and that he seemed to participate in and enjoy school so little. He made no response until she said one day that he almost acted as if he did not even go to school. He replied, "Well, I don't. That school—it isn't even there."

When this was reported by Jimmy's mother to his teacher, the teacher suggested that maybe Jimmy was afraid he would miss his mother too much if he really let all of himself come to school. And sure enough, after Jimmy's mother had talked this over with him, he did let his sad feelings come in separating from her and in wistfully looking after her when she left. He was able to cry one day after she left and could accept the teacher's comfort, sympathy, and support.

In his teacher's words, "Then he came alive for us." But Jimmy's story does not end so simply.

CHILD TESTS TEACHER

In a few weeks his old behavior of being absent in feeling, though present in body, returned, ushered in by a brief fit of temper on leaving his mother one day. The teacher observed this episode and astutely felt it was a fear attack. She mentioned to Jimmy that some children felt afraid away from home and mother, and maybe he felt that way, too. He made no response but played dangerously on the jungle gym in front of this teacher a few minutes later. She took him off the apparatus and told him spontaneously and very directly, "Jimmy, I think you're testing me to see if I'll keep you as safe at school as mother does at home." He tested a few more times, evoked the same response from his teacher, and then returned to being in school with feeling.

When all these events were reported back to me at a follow-up consultation on Jimmy, now a full-fledged, fully participating nursery schooler, we all congratulated ourselves on our brilliance and had a good discussion about the difference between separation feelings and separation problems. Jimmy was an excellent case in point for this distinction. When he came to school he evinced no separation feelings either at home or at school: he had shown no apprehension about the strange new school with its strange new people and strange new ways; he had shown no sadness whatsoever on leaving his beloved mother. Separation feelings should accompany starting school just as surely as cream is a part of milk. In our modern culture we may homogenize milk or artificially separate the cream just as we sometimes can artificially mask or deny the anxiety and sadness that must accompany a small child's separating from his mother.

But when Jimmy did not show to his teachers any of his separation feelings, it would not be proper to say he had a separation problem until two more steps were taken. First, we had to make sure the feelings he had not shown at school had not been shared with his mother unbeknownst to his teachers. And second, we had to find evidence that Jimmy had adopted ways of avoiding, warding off, or defending himself from these feelings, ways that interfered with his usual functioning. Both these conditions were fulfilled with Jimmy: his mother, too, had seen no evidence of any separation feelings; and, of course, Jimmy's feeling of absence at school had precluded his deriving any benefit from his first school experience.

If we but briefly review Jimmy's story to date, we can capitalize on the distinctions which I hope have been made clear, distinctions which I think are helpful in thinking about separation. First, Jimmy showed so clearly the difference between physical separation from his home and mother, which he achieved so readily, as contrasted with true mastery of at least part of the separation experience, which he achieved so slowly and which required such a great deal of effort on everyone's part. Second, he showed us the contrast between the average expectable separation feelings, his sadness and fears, and a separation problem. In the latter instance he used defenses (his massive denial of his school's existence) to ward off the separation feelings, defenses whose interference with his total functioning enabled us to speak of Jimmy's having had a separation problem or symptom at the start of school.

There are two more chapters to Jimmy's story. I am sure that those of you who have helped a child truly master a separation experience in starting school have been keenly aware of one glaring omission from the separation feelings so far mentioned. The usual triad of feelings is sadness, fear, and anger, and Jimmy's anger toward his mother for letting him go to school, for letting him leave her, and for exposing him to the unpleasant sadness and fear had so far been missing.

His teachers searched for it in his school behavior, but all in vain. They wondered if perhaps they had missed it in his temperlike outburst that had offered the entrée to discussing his fear at school; they wondered if, perhaps, this was a feeling that young Jimmy had somehow mastered silently by himself, although they knew this would be expecting more of his development than anyone had a right to expect. In retrospect, we were all remiss in not actively pursuing this quest a bit further, for sure enough, in due course, the anger made itself manifest.

ONSET OF NIGHT PROBLEMS

A few months after the sadness and fear had seemed mastered, with Jimmy still maintaining his full participation in school, the teachers began to be aware that Jimmy and his mother were being progressively just a bit later to school each day. In addition, Jimmy was rather a sleepy, tired, cranky boy by the end of the morning and his mother was beginning to look a bit worn out herself.

The head teacher finally quite tactfully took up the

lateness with the mother at the point when Jimmy was missing about half an hour at the start of each day. The mother then told of a most difficult night problem which had been going on for about two months. Jimmy dawdled and delayed in going upstairs, in getting ready for his bath, in bathing, in getting on his pajamas, and then, when finally in bed, would begin an interminable series of trips to the bathroom or downstairs to ask his mother or father rather tedious questions that could well have waited until the next day. Any gentle or firm insistence that he stop the nonsense and get into bed had been met with rather severe yelling, screaming temper outbursts.

The teacher at once recognized that his anger about leaving his mother to start school had been moved to home to make its appearance when he had to leave her to go to bed. The teacher chided the mother a bit for not having told her of this difficulty that, in timing, seemed so clearly connected with really working through his starting of school. The mother was rather confused and said she felt this had been a home problem that was hers to work out and could have had nothing to do with school since it had not occurred there. Actually, I rather doubt if the teacher would have chided the mother quite so much if she had not felt herself remiss for not asking about the appearance at home of the feelings, whose absence we had so directly noted and wondered about at school.

With but a little help from the teacher, after the original connection had been made, the mother was able to help Jimmy by pointing out that his angry feelings at bedtime had started just when they had begun to talk about his feelings about starting school, and that she felt he had been angry for weeks, not about leaving her to go to bed, but rather about leaving her to go to school. Jimmy heard her out very attentively before demanding,

"Well, what do you do all morning at home with the baby?" The mother immediately took up his obvious feeling that she sent him away to school so she could stay all morning at home with his baby brother, and assured him of how much she missed him and how she sent him to school to get him ready for kindergarten so he could grow up to be the big schoolboy he so wanted to be.

The night disturbance did not stop in a night or a week, but did subside gradually over the course of the ensuing month. But again Jimmy had been most instructive in two important ways. First, he reaffirmed, as I think we all need constant reaffirmation, that there is a triad of feelings involved in separation and that we cannot feel the job has been accomplished until all three have come to the surface in whatever manner and at whatever time they choose. And sometimes, with a child with very rugged defenses, they do not make themselves apparent, even during a second year in school. And second, Jimmy's case illustrates what has allowed separation feelings to go unnoticed so many times by school staff. The feelings do not show at school but rather at home, where the mother either does not connect them with school, or rather suffers them through, or works them through without telling the teachers what has transpired. For teachers who do not want to see or know about separation feelings these particular mechanisms in mother and child make it possible for the unsightly never to be seen.

RETURN OF DIFFICULTY WITH SEPARATION

The third chapter of Jimmy's story concerns his second year at school, when he was 4½. His teachers came back for a third consultation about him because they actually

doubted their very perceptive understanding of what was
going on with Jimmy.

The summer had gone rather unremarkably and
Jimmy had apparently eagerly returned to school. In fact
he had been so eager and controllable and so much in
love with his school that the teachers well recognized
what was going on. On arriving in the mornings when
his mother had done the driving, he rather rudely sent
her on her way home, interrupting one day a conversation
between his mother and teacher with, "Haven't you gone
yet?" He scorned the newly starting children whose mothers were sometimes spending the morning at the school,
helping their children to start. He was clearly the master
of the situation now except that he was a rather cruelly
bossing master, so often just curtly dismissing his mother.
Only a few times did this behavior change, and at these
times he would ask his mother's help with his coat or
boots and then require many minutes of her help with
tasks he could do on his own in a matter of seconds.

But the real difficulty came at the end of the day,
when Jimmy kept his mother waiting forever while he
finished this project or that one, or took forever getting
on his coat. When she would urge him to hurry up he
would become cross with her or would explain how much
fun he was having at school or how much he enjoyed it
and hated to leave.

The teachers recognized this collection of defenses
very well and it seemed to them that Jimmy was having
separation trouble again. They were very familiar with
the child who turns it all around, who is not left in the
morning by his mother but rather works it out so that he
leaves her; the child who does not wait all morning for
his mother to come but rather makes her wait for him at
the end of the school session; the child who is not missing
his home and beloved mother but rather only has some

trouble in leaving his beloved school and teachers. I do not believe any collection of defenses is more calculated to reduce a mother to feeling worthless and unneeded than these; and, of course, this is correct, as these are the feelings that Jimmy preferred that his mother feel rather than himself.

STRIKING DIFFERENCES APPEAR

All this was most familiar to his teachers who now asked how they could be right as they had worked through his separation feelings last year. How could all this be coming back all over again? From my point of view as an analyst this was all most instructive and interesting, and the teachers were able to see what fascinated me so much. Yes, Jimmy's separation feelings were giving him trouble again, but there were some striking differences.

The first of these was that rather than warding off these feelings with the immature, crippling denial of a year ago, a defense mechanism characteristic of a much younger child, Jimmy was using new defenses, more active, more age-appropriate, and less crippling ones. I told the teachers I would have been disheartened if the same old defenses had reemerged, but that I was not disturbed that the same old feelings were causing trouble, particularly when they were dealt with and contained in so much more healthy a way.

Finally, there is a crucial aspect of his teacher's report. When they had told Jimmy that it looked as if he was turning everything around so he would not need to have those old leaving mother feelings again, the feelings had rather easily become available to him and he rather easily surrendered his bossy controlling of his mother and his turning everything around. This lack of rigidity in his defenses, this fluidity that allowed his feelings to emerge from behind them with just essentially a few interpretations of the defenses, speaks for a great strength of Jimmy's personality. He was now master of his character and feelings and not they of him. This in contrast to the preceding year, when many days and weeks of work were necessary before he could stop his pretense that his school was not there.

This episode at the start of Jimmy's second year at school did start me thinking, as I began to wonder why it is that these separation feelings, as I have called them, seem to give many people so much difficulty and why it is we find ourselves working and reworking them over and over again. I felt this was a worthwhile line of thinking to pursue because I felt if I could understand a bit more about this I might better be able to help teachers with their frustrations and disappointments in helping children and parents with separations.

Actually, the term *separation feelings* is misleading and inaccurate. Although it is advantageous to contrast separation feelings with separation problems or symptoms, and is helpful in explaining about the average expectable response for a small child in leaving his mother, in fact we are dealing in our triad with much more than feelings. It is true that sadness is an affect and that it is involved in the separation. But the fear is in reality an anxiety which may have its roots in the child being afraid his instincts will overwhelm him without the controlling presence and support of his mother; or the child may be apprehensive that his aggressive feelings to his mother will turn out to be stronger than his loving ones. There may be other sources, although the two I have mentioned are, I believe, the most common. So when we are dealing with what we have called a child's separation fear we are actually directing our attention to some vital aspects of his personality: What is his tolerance for anxiety? What ways does he have available for dealing with anxiety? What is the balance between his loving and hating feelings or, said differently, how has he mastered the ambivalent conflicts of his anal sadistic phase of development? How secure does he feel his control is over his instincts?

COPING WITH FEELINGS

And when we come to his separation anger we really are not just dealing with one more feeling but are, in reality, directing our attention to how a child copes with a direct manifestation of one of his instincts, his aggressive drive.

So in dealing with what we have called separation feelings we are dealing in reality with how a child copes with feeling, with anxiety, with instincts, and with the balances between his defenses and his drives. We could not be getting in condensed form a more complete assessment of his personality growth and development and of his current emotional status. For if a child can cope appropriately in each of these areas, he will indeed have reached or achieved a most enviable state of emotional health. In assisting a child to master the separation from his mother in starting preschool, therefore, we are in fact evaluating and supporting the maturation of vital areas of his personality, expecting and helping him to attain what could be a remarkable degree of maturity.

When separation is viewed in this way, then two helpful points of view become quite clear. Complete mastery is rather like complete maturity, something for which we all aspire but perhaps never fully attain. And second, since we do not expect instincts and affects ever to be extinguished or anxiety ever to be eliminated, so we cannot expect separation difficulties somehow completely to disappear. How many of us still to this day are not free of sadness, apprehension, and perhaps some irritability at times of leaving loved ones or at any time of leaving. In this context we can feel we are being most realistic if we view the mastery of separation as a very gradual process which we try to assist a child in achieving bit by bit over the course of many experiences. But those who work with the young child in his first school experience, in his first true separation from his mother, if this be the case, have the opportunity for making this separation a healthy prototype for all the separations that will follow.

And this leads me to the final point that I would like to make. I think it must be clear that I am suggesting not only that preschool teachers give consideration to the possibility of approaching the mastery of feelings as an educational task properly belonging to the educationist's domain, but that this task can most profitably and wisely be initiated in dealing with the feelings that accompany the child's separation at the starting of school. I want to suggest that, rather than viewing the mastery of separation feelings as an insurmountable task or ordeal for preschool teachers, this situation may present an incomparable opportunity to the teachers. I can think of few more promising situations in which to effect the maximum in mental health, hygiene, or prophylaxis.

In what I have abstracted of Jimmy's story I have tried to show three different levels of work that a preschool teacher could initiate according to her skills, interests, and opportunities for consultative support. It is possible some teachers can work on all three levels, some on two, others on just the first. It is possible some will progress in time and experience from one level to yet another. My plea would simply be that any step that is taken is a step forward and that, if no steps are taken, a golden opportunity is missed by default.

EDUCATIONAL HELP WITH STARTING SCHOOL

What are these three levels of work?

On the first, the school is established to create a milieu for mothers to work through separation feelings if they can. This would mean discussing separation with mothers before school starts, insisting on mother's presence for a few days at the school to insure a somewhat gradual separation, and eliminating or restricting for at least the 3-year-olds the use of nonmother transportation.

And here it might be pertinent to add a personal conviction derived from my experience in assisting mothers in working with their children's feelings as aroused by the separation at the start of schooling. Just as we expect the child to experience certain feelings, so I think his mother will experience certain feelings. I expect a mother to be anxious about how her child will measure up. I expect her to be sad in her missing of him and those phases of infancy and early childhood that starting school seem to bring to an end. My conviction is a rather simple one: until a mother has cried with her sadness of missing her child she will not be able to help him in dealing with any of his feelings associated with missing her. Sympathetic understanding of the mother's plight is crucial to any talk about separation.

On the second level, the teachers would, in addition, help the child in school to identify his feelings, to experience them, and to express them in words (Katan, 1961). Examples of this were given in the teacher's handling of Jimmy's fear of being at school and in her acceptance of his sadness at missing his mother. It is most important in this regard always to tell the child, in encouraging him to put his feelings into words, that, "I don't know how mother wants you to manage it at home, but at school we want you to tell us, to say it when you are angry." This is necessary to obviate the impossible problem that ensues if a child learns to verbalize aggression or any other feeling at school, takes his newly found ability home only to find that his family cannot tolerate it. The limitations to this work that are imposed, if the parents cannot actively support and participate, have greatly increased our interest, here in Cleveland in work on the next level.

On this third level, the teachers would assist the mother in understanding and dealing with the child's feelings, perhaps even his defenses, helping her to assist him at home as well in identifying, experiencing, and putting them into words.

And now briefly to review the thoughts about the preschooler's separation at the starting of school that I hope have emerged. In following the story of Jimmy, I have tried to illustrate first, the difference between achieving physical presence at school and achieving mastery of the separation experience; second, the difference between separation feelings and a separation problem or symptoms; third, two of the most common defenses preschoolers may adopt—the absenting himself as regards his feelings that Jimmy first utilized, and the controlling reversing he used the next year; fourth, some of the reasons for and the means of approaching the management of the preschool child in separation experience.

I imagine there may be some who would say that the assistance to the mother and child which I have described Jimmy's teacher as offering is something that is really a bit beyond the training, interest, ability, and time of a nursery school teacher. It may be felt that there are too many concerns about staff and staffing, planning, economics, logistics, and all those other things that absorb a teacher's or director's time and energy.

In response to these thoughts, I offer the following. Jimmy's teacher stayed in her teacher's role throughout the work with Jimmy and his mother, because she had taken as part of her educational task or role, educating about feelings and their management. She has felt, as have many, that this greatly enhanced her success in the traditional educational role. With Jimmy there would have been no education in the traditional sense without the work with his feelings. I feel that the work she was able to do in her role as teacher enabled her to do a job in prophylactic psychiatry that no one else could possibly have achieved as simply and effectively as she did.

I would also suggest that it is not necessary to work through each aspect of separation with each child and mother, something which is blatantly impossible. Besides, some mothers will want no part of such efforts. But if your school creates a milieu in which a mother on her own may assist her child, just by doing this you will support some parents in such a way as to enable them to see a task they might otherwise not have noticed. In some instances, with just this support they will be able to accomplish some things that otherwise would not have been approached. If, in addition, the teacher can discuss separation feelings with mothers before the start of school, support will be extended to a few more; and all this without being involved directly with the mastery of feelings, or in anything remotely connected with psychiatry or therapy.

And certainly, most valuable will be any example the teacher sets of first helping a child in identifying his feelings, and then in allowing feelings to be expressed in words. In some instances a teacher might want to try to work more actively with the mothers. In all probability this will require either psychoanalytic consultation or further training, or both. If such facilities are unavailable in an area steps may have to be initiated in order to make them available. A nursery school's close, ongoing working relationship with a mental health professional may also prove useful in other ways. For example, approaching separation, as I have discussed it, will inevitably lead to the uncovering of children who are unable to cope and who will not be able to start school. In such instances, however, the teacher will have performed an important service in detecting a child who needs a referral for psychiatric evaluation.

Finally, and most importantly, whatever the teacher can reasonably achieve, considering the available facilities, in assisting with the mastery of separation as it becomes apparent in the preschool setting will be all to the good. The more that can be accomplished the better, but whatever a teacher accomplishes, no matter how little it may seem to be, is better than not having accomplished anything.

Chapter 4

Stress in the Nursery School

Erna Furman

A stress is a situation which imposes a special hardship. To master it, a personality has to muster more than its usual resources. It is often difficult to delineate a stress and even more difficult to specify its exact contents. It has to be seen within the context of the individual personality who is undergoing a certain experience at a certain time in his life. What constitutes a stress for one person, may be a traumatic experience for another, or a mere minor exertion for a third.

We are very familiar with this in regard to physical stress. The other day a woman told me of a middle-aged friend of hers: "Mary got new cross-country skis, so she spent all of last Sunday with a sports group skiing over hill and dale. By the end of the expedition she had to be carried home, and of course spent the rest of the week laid up with terrible muscle pains and totally worn out. Can you imagine doing such a foolish thing? A person of her age, with no skiing experience and used to spending the day at the office!" I agreed, of course; I too knew that a person's ability to take in stride such a stress depends on his age, his general body makeup, and state of health, his current degree of exercise and muscle training, his detailed planning of the expedition in terms of food intake, rest periods, and so on. To the untrained at any age everything is a stress.

RECOGNIZING STRESSFUL SITUATIONS

With mental stress, we are all prone to act like the skiing Mary. The more stressful a situation may be, the more we tend to close our eyes to it, minimize its hardships, or even pretend to ourselves that it is a lark instead of a trial. Still, there are many stressful situations which we do acknowledge to ourselves and, on the basis of our own experience, are able to empathize with others in a similar plight. We know how it feels and we recognize in others the many signs that bespeak their distress, even when they do not tell us about it. We find it much harder, however, to empathize with a young child. All of us have essentially forgotten our preschool lives and feelings, and something in us takes good care to prevent us from remembering them. We cannot judge by our adult experiences what constitutes a stress for a child and we do not recognize the signs by which he shows his stress. This prevents us from sparing him certain stresses, from helping him cope with others, from knowing when he struggles with it successfully, and when he does not. As a result we also often neglect to train children for emotional stresses by helping them to develop those mental "muscles" that are essential for dealing with hardships, just as gradual and continual bodily exercise could have prepared Mary for her skiing trip.

Our already limited ability to understand a child's stress is even further handicapped when we somehow sense that we are the cause of his stress, or when we vaguely realize that we cannot shield him from it, or when his pain threatens to bring back memories of our own old forgotten childhood pains; in short, when his needs in one way or another are at cross-purposes with our own.

STRESSES INHERENT IN ATTENDING NURSERY SCHOOL

To start with, let me illustrate some of these points in relation to entry to nursery school. The chapter "On Separation at Entry to Nursery School" details some of the ways in which children and parents cope with the stress of taking this new developmental step and how teachers can help them master it. Many teachers can empathize with parent and child in this situation, appreciating that changes are always hard, that growing up often brings mixed feelings, and that a new setting is inevitably strange and a little scary. Most of us, however, shy away from recognizing that a child's upset may also be due to stresses engendered by the school itself, stresses that we impose upon the child even in the best of schools.

One of these stresses is the heightened risk of physical illness. Mothers often bring it to our attention because they bear the brunt of it. Suddenly the child is exposed to a much wider community, not only of people but of viruses and bacteria. It is not uncommon for a youngster during his first few months of nursery school to spend as many days at home sick as he spends at school well. It is often a painful, long process of gradual self-immunization. These sicknesses bring their own stresses for the child and leave him physically and emotionally weakened just when he most needs all his healthy resources at his disposal. No wonder that mothers and children blame the school for these new hardships. No wonder they become more critical of the school in general and sometimes even question the wisdom of attending nursery school at all.

Other school stresses are perhaps less obvious but no less severe: There is no doubt that even the most alert teacher cannot supervise a group of children as closely as, in the home setting, one mother can supervise one or very few children, all of whom she knows intimately. This is further exaggerated by the fact that nursery schools have different, and usually much more, equipment than is in the home. We think of jungle gyms, clay, paint, or woodworking tools as pleasurable and inviting materials which will motivate the child toward new interests and masteries, but it is also true that, to the newcomer especially, they are just more unfamiliar things to get into trouble with. The changed ratio of adult to children, combined with the multitude of new materials, represents a considerable element of lessened safety for the child. How can he feel protected and safe when there are so many opportunities for trouble and so much less of a grown-up to take care of him?

This reminds me of another stress the nursery school brings to the child, namely exposure to aggressive and unkind children, to fearful and upset children, to children with various behavior difficulties. They frighten a youngster when he is the actual or potential victim as well as when they simply impress him as strange and unreasonable; or when, by contrast, they remind him of feelings in himself which he has trouble mastering, such as fears, feelings of missing his mother, difficulty in sharing, impulses to mess, or to engage in bodily excitements. A "normal" group of nursery school children inevitably presents a wide variety of such manifestations and each affects the new child in a different manner or degree. Sometimes the threat of bodily disfigurement is added, when one of the children, teachers, or visiting parents has a physical anomaly, be it a congenital body defect or weakness, be it the evidence of sickness or injury, such as scars, casts, bandages, or be it injuries and illnesses that actually occur at school; for example, a bad fall, a mashed finger, an attack of asthma, or fainting.

The nursery school does not limit its stresses to adults' and peers' bodies and behaviors, it also forces upon the attention of the child many of the events that take place in the homes and lives of all these new people. Unavoidably, he learns of births, illnesses, deaths, hospitalizations, divorces, robberies, car accidents, family arguments, and many other upheavals which regularly befall at least some of the families in a nursery group in the course of a school year, and which, through direct conversations or through less direct behavioral changes in the affected children, enter the daily routine of the school. Even the trip to and from school and the location of the school itself expose the child to the many new experiences of the wider community which often include stressful events; for example, accidents, ambulances, demolition crews at work, or funeral processions. Some nursery schools are situated near hospitals, churches, or funeral homes whose activities draw the children's attention to the stresses of life. I know of several instances where teachers first tried to overlook such circumstances. The children did not talk about their observations, but they could not concentrate on school activities, their behavior was unsettled and erratic, they frequently stared out the windows or listened for outside sounds. Sometimes the content of their free play reflected some aspects of their concerns. When the teachers recognized the children's stress, they spent time and effort in discussing the children's ideas, explaining the realities, and helping the children come to terms with them. These weeks and months of painful, patient work paid off in enabling the children to focus their energies

on the school activities. They mastered the stress instead
of halfheartedly warding off its impact.

TOO MUCH STRESS IN THE NURSERY SCHOOL

Where we perhaps most often impose too much stress
on our pupils is in minimizing how important we are to
them, how much they count on us being there, and how
much their feeling safe and their ability to function well
depends on their relationship with us. As a result, we
may not sufficiently prepare them for our planned absences, may not familiarize them ahead of time with
whoever will temporarily take our place, and in the case
of unplanned absences, may not make sure that they are
discussed and helpfully explained in simple terms. Indeed, we sometimes act as though we expected the children not to notice these changes or not to find them
legitimately stressful and difficult to master without our
special help. The children may then comply by apparently
not noticing or caring and by not commenting or ques-
tioning in words; but their response tends to manifest
itself in diminished ability to concentrate, to follow rules,
to exercise self-control, and to get along with peers, not
to mention the proverbially difficult lot of the substitute
and of the "settling down" period which burdens the regular teacher on her return. We then sometimes scold the
children for their naughtiness, feel that their misbehavior was due to a case of "when the cat's away, the mice
play," and we perhaps also blame the substitute for not
imposing effective controls. In large part, however, the
children's difficulties simply indicate that they have been
faced with more than they could cope with. Most youngsters are much better able to take the change in stride
when they are helped with verbal preparation and given

opportunities to discuss their questions, concerns, and feelings.

To a lesser but still significant extent, this applies to helping children master the stress of visitors in the classroom. Even we adults would feel uncomfortable, perhaps afraid or suspicious, and at least intruded upon, if a stranger appeared in our school unannounced, did not introduce himself, and failed to inform us as to the purpose of the visit. Children are very observant, and we encourage them to be. They also feel as we do about strangers, but their attitude to them is not yet as realistic as that of adults. They may be unduly wary of strangers or unduly familiar and forthcoming with them, and sometimes this latter behavior actually serves to ward off their anxiety, as if they are saying, "If I am very nice to you, you won't hurt me." In either case, we can only teach children how to behave with strangers by demonstrating sensible ways of assessing what they are about. Thus, we would offer them the very means we use: being prepared for their arrival if possible, being mutually introduced, and understanding why they have come. For example, "They are a mommy and daddy who came to look at our school to see if it's the right school for their little boy"; or, "This lady is learning to be a teacher and that's why she will be here to watch how we teach and learn in our school." Some children then feel free to get on with their own business, others may need to question the teacher or visitor further. In one preschool, the official from the accreditation bureau paid a surprise visit, was briefly introduced, and seated herself in the corner of the room. Pretty soon the teacher noticed a change in the atmosphere. It was strangely quiet, all the children had congregated into the far block area and were busy erecting a wall that effectively isolated them from the guest. The teacher realized that something was troubling the children and she suddenly put two and two together: It was Halloween, the lady had dark hair, wore a black dress and boots—the children thought she was a witch! The teacher then talked with the children about their worry about the visitor, related perhaps to her sudden appearance, black outfit, and it being Halloween time. She went on to explain in some detail the purpose of the visit. There was a sigh of relief, many questions, and then normal play resumed.

Children are often similarly taken aback by changes which do not involve people, changes in the classroom arrangement of furniture and materials, changes in schedule, or in activities. They handle all of these better with preparation, explanation, and discussion which helps to clarify potential misunderstandings.

Sometimes we think that children really like at least nice surprises. Big, noisy birthday and holiday parties are considered treats for the children, and teachers may spend hours in advance preparing special surprises for such occasions. Little do we appreciate the overwhelming nature of such events for our young pupils. We may even mistake their excited shrieks, hyperactivity, and loud laughter for genuine enjoyment. We may take at face value their pleas for "When can we have another party?" (just as we used to think that little children enjoy a scary story because they ask for it to be read over and over). Yet, in other situations, such as peer play, we recognize that excited laughing and hyperactivity may thinly disguise inner turmoil due to upset, sadness, and anger, and that even pleasure, beyond a certain pitch of intensity, ends up in irritability or tears. We are also aware that the wish to have something repeated does not always stem from liking it but may be motivated by a need to have some active part in controlling the stress by repeating it at will, making it happen, and thereby avoiding being taken by surprise.

The situation is not much different when it comes to single field trips to unfamiliar places. A trip to the science museum or to a farm tends to be an overwhelming experience in which children need all their resources just to master the strangeness and multitude of impressions, so that little energy is left for learning something about the new place and integrating it into their store of knowledge. We as adults have of course taken such trips many times and therefore find them educational and enjoyable. It is difficult for us to appreciate just how hard it is for children to absorb excesses of stimuli. One farmer who frequently welcomed groups of preschoolers to his small barn, found that on their first visit most children learned next to nothing. Some ran around wildly, others hung back bewildered, others yet were disgusted by the smell and sight of the animals' excrements and declared the whole place "yukky." Similarly, at a suburban nature center, the preschoolers' first visit was either spent on their investigating the familiar—the toilets, water fountains, and snacks—or on the adults having to dispell their expectation of bears and poisonous snakes. One day care center's visit to a nearby vacant lot turned into a fiasco when the children feared to walk through the unfamiliar tall grass. Careful preparation, follow-up, and repeated visits enabled many of these children to reduce the influx of stimuli to manageable proportions, to familiarize themselves with the unknown, and to learn with pleasure from these experiences. I do not imply that we should not take field trips, but if we can learn to feel better with our children, we will spend a great deal of a year's curriculum in preparing for them and working them through afterwards. Our choice of trip will be adapted to the life experiences and background knowledge of our special nursery group, and we may try to choose a trip which can be repeated several times to help them master the experience.

I want to mention one other area where we often unwittingly impose too much stress on youngsters in preschool. It has to do with bodily privacy. Children's infantile curiosity about bodies, their own and others, is well known. Parents and teachers of young children also usually realize that this interest is not purely intellectual but rouses many feelings. Children are often pleasurably excited by looking at and showing off naked bodies, sexual, and excretory functions. They are also easily overstimulated as well as upset by what they perceive. At their stage of development, the intimacy of sharing toileting activities in bathrooms without doors or curtains, or of undressing in front of each other for naps or swims, tends to heighten their level of excitement and/or concern, and diminishes their resources for coping with other demands. This is especially true for children who have difficulty in being in charge of their feelings, or who are very excitable, or who in the nursery setting observe the differences between boys and girls for the first time. The intimate questions, feelings, and concerns about bodily matters are best dealt with in the home. At school we want to engage the child's curiosity in learning about other things and offer him opportunities to show off achievements instead of his naked body. Children's capacity to learn and understand depends on what and how much they have to absorb and on their feeling state. They cannot learn well when their feelings are too intense and threaten to overwhelm them—be it excitement, anger, fear, humiliation, or any other feeling. Several nursery schools and day care centers, unhappy about the children's general difficulty in "settling down," focusing on activities, and playing constructively with others, reported a significant change for the better when they instituted privacy—not secrecy—in toileting and undressing. Most children accepted the change readily and calmed down. A very few who showed special concerns by intruding upon others through peeking or exposing themselves could be helped in cooperation with their parents to explore and understand what bothered them.

In fostering personal privacy, as in a number of other areas, the preschool also helps children to prepare for and adapt to the rules of the wider community of which it is among the first representatives in the child's life. In this country, nudity, sexual practices, and toileting are legally prohibited in public, whereas families and private groups are left to manage these matters largely as they see fit.

TOO LITTLE STRESS IN THE NURSERY SCHOOL

Now let us look at some of the areas where we tend to impose too little stress. All of us consider social interactions an important area of learning in the nursery school. Most of us are quick to interfere when children hurt one another or destroy toys wantonly. Increasingly, teachers offer verbal anger as an alternate outlet and/or substitute materials; for example, newspapers to cut up or tear. It is relatively rare, however, that we expect and actively encourage children to be kind, thoughtful, and polite to adults and peers. I do not mean the use of the words *please* and *thank you* as magic tools for getting what you want, but as daily civil forms of interaction that make living together so much more pleasant. Although children at that age still find impulse control quite difficult, it is also a time when they wish to emulate the adults and when they take pride and pleasure in achieving adult aspects of behavior. We fail them when we lower our standards for them unduly in this area of social amenities, just as we would fail them if we omitted to teach other things they were ready for. Sometimes we encourage and appreciate their consideration and respect more with adults than with peers, or we expect these attitudes in their dealings with people but not with animals and plants. Although I certainly do not advocate our return to a multitude of empty social phrases, I do feel there is a place for a certain number of them. They help to smooth some situations and are often important building blocks toward delaying or substituting gratifications and thereby achieving better inner controls. The immediate rewards for the child are the admiration and love of others and a good feeling about himself in acting in a grown-up fashion. These somewhat superficial but helpful social amenities should of course go hand in hand with a consistent encouragement of pity and active concern for others, which often require the special help of the teacher.

Related to this area of too little stress are those of impulse control in general and of correcting mistakes and making up for damage or hurt. Our schools still expect too much in this area; for example, that children will sit quietly on a chair for a long period while waiting for food or as a punishment. More often, however, teachers feel that children need to let off steam by excited chasing games, messing with materials, or misuse of toys for mutual teasing. Even when we decide that a certain behavior needs to be stopped, we may talk to the child repeatedly in the form of gentle suggestions rather than in explicit, firm terms; or, when he has caused some damage, we often do not insist that he participate in repairing it. Perhaps with some justification, we act as though we, rather than the child, were to blame and that we, rather than he or she, were responsible for putting things right, be it comforting the hurt victim, mopping up the floor, taping the book, or sorting out the puzzle pieces. I do not suggest yelling orders or spanking offenders. I do suggest firm and direct expectations that are really meant, early interference when necessary, and resourcefulness and patience in helping children to take their part in making up damage that could not be prevented. Many infantile impulses, such as the wish to hurt, tease, grab, or mess, are not easier to control when they have been gratified. Each time we help children to refrain from such behavior they have a better chance to master it.

In the areas of interest and achievement in activities (what we often refer to as "real" learning), we also have a tendency to expect much too little of our pupils. We strive to provide as many enticing materials and activities as possible, but we are sometimes too little concerned when a child limits himself to a very few. On the one hand we know how important it is to help him broaden his interests, on the other hand we are content to leave him to a favorite pursuit to the exclusion of all else. Thus some children assiduously avoid painting, or large-muscle apparatus, or music. Others spend all their time with blocks or puzzles or in the doll corner. To some extent no doubt each child has his favorite activity and his special aptitude, and deserves the chance to enjoy and develop these. Many children, however, stick with one activity because it provides a false security. They avoid other activities for fear of failure, competition, or simply reluctance to try the less familiar. Unless we interfere judiciously, unless we encourage and sometimes insist that a child try his hand at different things for certain periods of the day, the opportunity to choose from a wide variety may be misused to foster a child's self-imposed restrictions. In observing a child work at a previously neglected or avoided activity we can often help him with a fear of being laughed at, or with a difficulty in self-esteem, or inability to bear the frustration of making mistakes.

Similarly, when children are engaged in activities, we sometimes fail them by not expecting sufficiently high standards of achievement. After a child has worked at the easel for some days and still produces the same blotches, he may find himself rewarded with the same genuine praise that met his first effort. No doubt only individual knowledge of the child can enable us to judge correctly when and whether he would profit from a demand for a change of design or color, a more sustained effort, a more meticulous technique. For each child, however, such a time comes, when he is more helped by an expectation of greater exertion on his part than by a repetition of praise for relatively little effort. Much has been said about mothers who constantly burden their children with excessive demands for achievement; perhaps too little has been said about parents and teachers who impair their children's personality development by challenging them too little. By setting our standards of achievement too low, or by not raising them constantly in accord with the child's capacity for growth, we are not treating our pupils kindly. By requiring a steady effort from them we not only impose some stress but also convey a feeling of trust in their capacities.

THE TEACHER'S ROLE IN FOSTERING MEANS OF MASTERY

By now it may seem that I expect nursery school teachers to be busy with nothing else but stress—either avoiding excessive stress, or helping master stress that cannot be avoided, or making situations more stressful than they are. Well, perhaps you are right. Consistent "mental muscle" training for stress is, I believe, one of the nursery school's most important educational provinces. Planning it, executing it, adapting it to the needs of the individual child, group, and situation, takes up much of the teacher's attention and energy. I shall not attempt to enumerate all the mental faculties that play a part in this "training," but shall briefly highlight a few by way of summary.

Realistic observation is probably the keystone. We usually encourage our pupils to use all their senses to perceive accurately what is going on around them and we point out instances where they have not paid enough attention or have allowed themselves to be deceived. We encourage this careful kind of observing particularly when we want to teach them how to master a potentially dangerous situation. "Be sure and look carefully both ways and listen for car noises," we tell them when we instruct them on how to cross the road. It would not make sense to say, "Just close your eyes, pretend you don't see or hear anything and run ahead. This way you won't be scared of card." Let us then not act as though we wanted them to pretend that they had not seen the dead bird in the play yard, that they had not heard Johnny talk about his uncle's car accident, had not perceived the scar on Mary's mother's arm, or the visitor at the door. Let us, likewise, not act as though we wanted them to pretend that they had not experienced sadness, anger, fright—the realities inside themselves.

The next important step is verbalization, the tool by which observations are formulated. Words are the unique mental symbols that help us to confirm and order our impressions, to give them coherence as well as making them distinct. Talking, by both teacher and child, is essential in order to pinpoint and share observations as well as to question and to explain. In this way, observation and verbalization lead to distinguishing reality from fantasy, to understanding the logical sequences of cause and effect, and to assimilating the new and strange by comparing it with the familiar and known, and gradually integrating it into the world of experiences.

All these faculties which are so essential to mastery are still poorly developed in the young child. All of them require the teacher's assistance and support. Similarly, immature in the child, but essential to mastery, are those faculties which enable us to bear internal stress, either by itself or as the inevitable accompaniment of stress outside ourselves; for example, such faculties as the ability to bear anguish and frustration, the ability to wait for the fulfillment of our wishes, to give them up altogether, or to accept less satisfactory substitues, to see ourselves as diffferent from others, and at other times, to feel with them. The daily opportunity to develop, exercise, and use these faculties with the help of an understanding teacher can make a very considerable contribution to a young child's growing ability to cope with daily stresses in a healthy fashion and to prepare himself for some of the bigger stresses which life inevitably brings.

Chapter 5

Discipline

Erna Furman

PART I. ON PREVENTING DISCIPLINARY PROBLEMS

Let me start by describing a disciplinary problem which I experienced many years ago. I had already worked for a number of years, teaching and caring for school-aged children. I then changed jobs and went to look after younger children, 4- and 5-year-olds in a residential nursery for disturbed children. It was a family-like setting; the children were in groups of five, with a group mother in charge practically all the time, except for her 2 hours off a day. During those 2 hours I, as the newcomer, took one of the groups for a little walk along a route which the children knew well from many previous excursions. It was a nice day in a lovely rural setting. We set off and all went quite well at first. As we began to head back, however, first one child disappeared into a toolshed he had spied on the way, and then another followed him. I was very afraid of what might be in the toolshed but I had three other children to take care of; I called to the runaways sternly but without avail. Soon the third child took off, and when we came to a stream

69

the last two deserted me, dashing down to the water.
There was nothing I could do. They did not heed my calls;
if I went to get one, another one would run away. At first
I stood still, and then I walked slowly homeward. I felt
deeply humiliated and very unhappy. Eventually all five
children caught up and we arrived back on time, perhaps
because they did not want to miss their snack. Nothing
major had happened; but that was to their credit, not to
mine. I could not tell the group mother all that had transpired because I was too ashamed.

When you come up against a situation like this you
can either give up teaching or you can start to work on
it. The first thing I noticed was that the group mother
had no difficulty with these children. She talked to them
much as I had done, and they did what they were expected
to do, most of the time. So it was clear my trouble had
nothing to do with not using the right words or the right
tone. The children misbehaved with me because they did
not know me and I did not really know them. It was as
simple as that. With young children the relationship between the adult and the child is absolutely vital to the
adequate functioning of their personalities. It provides
the necessary safe framework and supports all the child
has ever learned, including his capacity to be "good."
Having understood this helped me, in later years, to dis-
suade substitutes from going on walks. Instead, I encouraged them to remain in the most familiar and
structured setting until they developed a relationship
with the children. The relationship, the truly knowing
and liking each other, is not the only thing that makes
things tick, but it is an essential.

I learned another lesson from my sorry experience.
Fortunately, these children, like most 4- and 5-year-olds,
had reached the level of development at which they recognized common dangers. They appreciated that they had

been told not to go into the stream, and not to handle the farm tools in the shed, in order to keep safe, rather than because these were their group mother's whims. Luckily for me, they had been helped to know that one follows rules because they are intended to protect one's own and other people's safety.

It took a long time before I understood yet another reason why nothing worse had happened on my walk with them. *I* was determined not to tell very much about the events on the walk, but the children told *everything* in detail to their group mother at snack time. I was mortified but also very interested. I did not understand their motive at first. They did not tattle on me. They told all because *they* felt like bad children. They wanted to ease their consciences by letting her know that they had been bad. She duly fulfilled the task they had assigned to her—she told them off. Their just developing consciences demanded that they confess and be scolded. Their inner monitors were not yet fully effective in helping them to behave well, but had perhaps prevented them from acting worse than they did.

Many years later, when I was preparing this discussion, my own children asked me what I was working on and I told them. My children were then in early puberty and late school age, so I suggested they help by telling me what made them behave well at school. They thought it through and mentioned the same three points which I have just brought up. Only, since they are much older than underfives, they put them in the reverse order: first, "So I won't feel bad"; second, "So I'll be safe"; third, "Because I kind of like the teacher and want her to like me." As adults, we probably would not bother with the relationship aspect at all. For me, behaving properly is mainly a matter of my conscience and of my sense of reality and safety. The farther down we go in the age

groups, however, the more are these aspects reversed, so
that the relationship matters most to the youngest children.

The Role of the Relationship

Let us now look more closely at each of these aspects,
focusing first on the role of the adult–child relationship.
At the time of entry to nursery school, children find themselves alone in a new setting. With many this leads to
one or another disciplinary problem. Now I am not thinking of major psychiatric disease, I mean spilling the milk,
knocking over somebody's block building, refusing to
come to story time, not listening to instructions, in short,
the many minor misbehaviors a teacher encounters all
day long. At home these children behave, in so far as they
do behave, because they are fond of their parents and feel
loved by them. They feel safe knowing that they are loved,
and act so as to preserve that love. When they first come
to school, they experience a vacuum. There is no adult
they care for or who knows them enough to love them.
Why then don't they all run wild? Most of them, after all,
are quite good, especially at first. When a young child
leaves the person he most cares for, he may handle his
feelings of unsafety and lack of support in many different
ways. He may feel unsafe inside, fearing loss of inner
control, or unsafe outside, fearing that the teacher and
peers could be very mean to him. He may, and usually
does, feel a mixture of both these fears. We see them
manifested in various forms of behavior. We see the children who come into school boasting, "I'm the big guy. I
can beat anybody here." They may even put their threats
into action, obviously terrified that somebody will beat
them up and using offense as the best defense. Others
deal with their fear by being initially very subdued and

listless or restricted in their activities. Some cling to
mother and try to protect themselves through her, and
others cling to the teacher in the hope that she is going
to be like mother. A few children are just anxious and
clumsy and cannot listen to anything they are told. We
can often understand what a child feels but there is not
much a teacher can do to change this right away. It is
not the teacher's fault that some children do not behave
well when they first come to school and, in so far as they
do behave, it is not to the teacher's credit. It takes time
before we can build our relationships with children and
help them fill the unsafe vacuum. Let us discuss some of
the steps by which we try to achieve it. You mostly know
these steps already from your work.

I have found it most useful to bridge the gap; that is,
the period after the children leave their parents and before they have made a relationship with me, by "extending" their parents into the school as much as possible. I
talk a great deal about their parents and ask them about
their parents to remind them of home and to help them
bring the parents' love to school, at least in their minds.
In connection with routines and activities I often ask
them to tell me how they do it at home. Also, before school
starts and during the first weeks and months, I try to get
the parents' approval for school rules. There are many
parents who find it very difficult to accept differences in
home and school rules. Some say, "If you have trouble
with Johnny at school, that's your own fault. You should
whip him and then he'll behave because that's what he's
used to." Other parents do not like some of the toys and
materials we use; for example, they object to certain kinds
of jungle gyms or to the use of paint. They don't state
directly to teacher or child, "You shouldn't paint at
school," instead, they complain that Johnny came home
with paint on his pants. Or they reproach their child for

getting dirty. The implication in either case is that as parents, they do not approve of things being done differently at school. It is an understandable feeling which I, as a parent, often share. But I think it helps if the teacher discusses with parents, and with child and parents, that some things have to be different at school and why. We do not expect the parents always to alter their rules, we just hope they will approve what we do at school as appropriate for school. Such acceptance helps the child to feel that the parents' good will, love, and support accompany him at school, that he can enjoy participating at school without risking parental disapproval.

There are many other ways in which one can bring the parent into the school: by sending things home to the parent and by welcoming things and ideas children bring from home. In the process of talking about the parents and home we also build a relationship with the children. When the teacher talks, and listens to the child's talk about his family, the child begins to feel she is a friend who wants to know things about his life. Sometimes children do not tell pleasant things. We hear about frightening or embarrassing events quite often, but they are all part of the child's life and are meaningful to him. As a friend, I want to learn about them too. I want to listen sympathetically, even if I do not always comment much, and often indeed cannot help.

There are other ways in which we establish relationships. We praise work, we praise good behavior, we show interest in the child's activities. Most of all, I think, we establish a relationship by helping children believe that we are there to keep them safe, that it is our job, first and foremost, to make sure that this new school is safe and that they are safe in it. I tell the children so in no uncertain terms. The first time I see a child get into a bit of trouble with another child, I separate them and I stress the fact that I have to keep each child safe, that I do not let children hurt anybody, and I do not let anybody hurt them. I cannot always enforce this. Sometimes things happen behind my back. But these mistakes are overcome without shattering the children's confidence, as long as the teacher herself does not treat them as major tragedies. If my belief in myself is shaken because I have not been able to prevent this or that incident, the child senses my lack of inner confidence and accepts it as his own, "She doesn't believe she can keep us safe. How could I do any better?" This tension can spread, and one mishap can lead to many more. I realize the foolishness of advising a teacher to trust herself and the children will trust her, or telling her that the way to make a child feel safe is to have confidence in herself in spite of things that go wrong, in spite of mistakes and setbacks. Self-confidence always comes harder for some than for others, and nobody has it all the time. Maybe we can keep trust in ourselves as teachers a little bit better when we appreciate that the child's misbehavior, particularly in the beginning of school, but to some extent always, is not the end of the world or even the end of our reputation as teachers. We make mistakes, we acknowledge and correct them, then we go on to the next thing with the will and expectation to work as best we can toward our goals.

The Role of Rules

Let us now turn to the second of our three aspects, the role of rules. There are some rules which even 4- and 5-year-old children respect—at least most of them do. But there are many rules which they do not consider as being to their advantage, and there are many more rules which they don't keep at certain moments. For example, when it comes to crossing the street, a 4- or 5-year-old has generally matured enough so that, in contrast to the 2-year-old, he is aware of the danger of cars and does not heedlessly dash into traffic. The street with traffic is a form of common danger nursery school children have learned to avoid. They know that "look before you run" is a rule intended for their safety. There are, however, times when the 4- or 5-year-old finds it impossible to keep even a rule he accepts. I am thinking of a little boy who has waited and waited at the front door to be picked up; suddenly he catches a glimpse of his mother across the street and—dashes toward her. We would not think of such an incident as breaking a rule willfully, nor would we think that he does not know this rule in terms of his own safety. We take it for granted that a young child cannot consistently stick even to the rules he knows and respects.

There are other rules that children do not recognize at all. For instance, many schools have a rule against running in the corridors. I have never found a youngster who understood that this had anything to do with his safety, even though it was clearly explained. Despite explanations, children are apt to think that not running in corridors is a rule because the director does not want to be disturbed, because the teacher does not like to run herself, and thinks she will not be able to catch up with them, or because she likes to spoil their fun. One of the major tasks of the nursery school and kindergarten teacher is to help children learn that rules are not personal whims, that rules are not obeyed because adults get cross or because some terrible punishment will be meted out, but that rules are there to help keep everyone safe. It is a very hard teaching task.

I start with it as soon as a child enters school. At that time there usually is an opportunity to explain the differences between home rules and school rules. Some children feel that rules at school are much more relaxed than rules at home, that you can pursue many more activities, make much more noise, climb on things, play with sand and paint, and do all these things that mothers do not like in their living rooms. This sometimes leads them to think that school has no rules, that it is a place where everything goes. For this reason, one of the first things I try to clarify for the children is that it is not true that we do not have any rules, we just have different rules and they are rules their parents accept as okay for school. It takes much time and talk for children to learn that there are differences in rules, that rules are for basic safety, that different rules does not mean no rules, and much of this discussion is initiated by the teacher.

Being a child means, for the most part, having to accept safety measures from outside because he has very few, as yet, inside himself. The child lives in a world of rules imposed by others. This often makes children feel helpless and angry, and this in turn makes it even harder for them to keep the rules. We can help them by keeping rules to a minimum. Each rule must be introduced at a time when it is essential, it must be explained, it must be enforced consistently, and it *will* work. But then suddenly, a new teacher, parent, or child may question an "essential" rule. And to the teacher's amazement, she realizes that she has accumulated a whole bunch of rules which have long outlived their usefulness and now just clutter up her own and her pupils' lives. Though I try to keep rules to the basic minimum, they have a way of accumulating like the contents of an attic which should be discarded at regular intervals. We need to keep this in mind when someone asks us what a certain rule is for. We tend to feel hurt because this is our own rule and we, or our establishment, have gotten attached to it. In truth,

the questioner often has a point, because rules constantly
need to be reevaluated.

The Role of Self-Esteem and Conscience

The third aspect of preventing disciplinary problems
is the one we adults put first: We do the right thing
because we cannot live with ourselves when we do the
wrong thing. We behave correctly in order to avoid a
guilty conscience. It often amazes me how much we un-
derestimate this aspect. We readily claim that people
steal because there are not strict enough punishments for
theft. We forget that we ourselves do not steal although
we are subject to the same "lenient" laws. Actually we
do not steal because we would not like ourselves, even if
nobody found us out. When we ask children why they
walk around Johnny's blocks rather than into them, they
usually say it's because they did not want to get in trouble. When we ask them further, "Supposing nobody had
seen you?" they sometimes add very reluctantly "Well,
it's not right."

Young children, even more than grown-ups, do not
like to look at their conscience. Of course, their conscience
is not yet fully established and is not a reliable guide to
them, but also they do not want to look at their early
conscience because they so often fail to come up to its
demands and because it is such a very harsh taskmaster.
For young children it is a very new experience to realize
that something is talking to them inside. They find it
unfamiliar and unpleasant and do all they can not to
listen to their "inner voice." Like my little charges on our
walk of many years ago, they prefer to act as though
mother or teacher were the conscience ("We'll tell her
and then she can scold us"). Chances are that mother and

teacher scold much less, however cross they may be, than one's own conscience, which seems to scold forever.

Another way children avoid pangs of conscience is to make sure that everybody *else* behaves well. They tell other children what to do and point out every lapse. They are veritable caricatures of teachers. And they also deal with a guilty conscience by tattling on others. In the nursery age group tattling is different from that of older schoolchildren. It is the young child's attempt to come to terms with his conscience. I remember Henry, a great tattler, always coming to tell me who had done what. All I had to reply was, "Henry, has there been something that you have done wrong? You sound to me like you feel bad inside." Then we would soon find what he had done wrong. Young children's tattling often means they wish it was not them who was so bad, or that at least they are not the *only* one that is bad. I therefore take their tattling as a way of letting me know that they feel bad and I try to help them recognize this.

There are many ways in which a teacher can use the child's beginning conscience as an ally in helping him to behave well at school and to use his conscience as a guide for himself. I usually remind children that if they do things right they will feel good about themselves. I do not stress that *I* am so pleased, but rather how good the *child* must feel that he has managed to play in the block corner without fighting. Unless we remind the child to look and to listen inside himself, he is not apt to be aware of what it is that is going on inside of him, that can help him do the correct thing and make him like himself. When a child appears unable to notice himself misbehave, I sometimes ask, "If you were the teacher and saw a boy throwing his clothes all around the room, what would you think?" Often this helps a child to engage in some self-observation. Time and again they are then quite crit-

ical of their own behavior. Another way in which we can
sometimes help a child to step back and look at and into
himself, is by witholding our judgment for a while, and
asking him what *he* thinks, how does it make *him* feel.

The teacher can take it for granted that the nursery
school and kindergarten child knows most dos and don'ts,
even when he cannot live up to them, and even when he
denies his failures and guilt. In time the teacher can help
him recognize his own inner standards and become less
dependent on adult admonition and correction. After all,
what we most want to achieve is not that children should
not be a trouble to us in the classroom—we want that
too—but we mainly want them to learn what *self*-disci-
pline is because it rests on a true recognition of the reality
and of its hazards, as well as on the guide of one's own
conscience. When our preschoolers leave us for elementary school they are not going to have reached this final
goal but, with our help, they may be a little closer to it.

PART II. WHAT TO DO WHEN PREVENTION HAS NOT WORKED

I do not think that anyone who has worked with, or
lived with, underfives, would think it strange that a second and equal part of any discussion on discipline should
be devoted to what to do when prevention has not worked.
All of us take it for granted that in living and working
with preschoolers, the best method, the best teacher, and
the best children cannot avoid trouble.

Often we do not give enough time and energy in our
schedules of working with children to dealing with this
aspect, and, as a result, when things do go wrong we tend
to feel pressured and regard mishaps and misbehaviors
as untoward interferences.

Teachers Get Angry Too

There is something else we all know and take for granted but do not make allowance for, namely, that when things go wrong we, the nursery school teachers, get angry, just like the parents, just like everybody else who works hard with an underfive to avoid trouble but then finds trouble everywhere. Sometimes it is a minor incident during a good day and we feel but a slight annoyance. Sometimes it is a bad day, lots of things go wrong, and we get very angry. We vary in the ways we respond, from person to person and time to time. We should make allowance for ourselves when we get angry. We should not only allow ourselves to feel angry but I think there are many situations where it is appropriate to let the child know he has made us angry, or that what he is doing is making us angry. If it is a minor annoyance we do not need to go over it with the child, but if we find ourselves getting very angry, I think it is helpful and realistic to tell the child so. This helps us to get on with the business, get beyond our anger, and shows the child how he can deal with his anger. Very often we cannot get on with the business at hand because we use up all our energy trying so desperately not to be angry or not to show anger. The longer the day goes on and the more things go wrong, the harder it is not to get angry.

Sometimes even a single incident makes us so unduly angry that we really cannot see beyond it. This was brought home to me once by our little neighbor boy Billy, 3½ years old at the time. He ran crying through his yard and into ours, and we asked him what the trouble was. "My Daddy spanked me," sobbed Billy. "Why did he spank you?" "My Daddy was angry." Billy had assessed the situation correctly. Anger ruled his father that day and anger was all Billy could see and comprehend. The precipitating event seemed to have little to do with it and, in any case, neither of them could address it. I have often wondered why we get, not just angry, but so unduly, so overwhelmingly angry at children. I think one reason is that, unbeknownst to us, we set ourselves, and cling to, some very unrealistic ideals. Although we know better, we feel that the perfect educator and the perfect method could really prevent the wrongdoings, the transgressions of rules, the naughtinesses, the misbehaviors. So when they do happen, they affect us not just as inevitable nuisances but as insults added to injury. It is as though we had failed. The more we remind ourselves that the children's naughtiness is not a reflection on us, that nobody could or should be able fully to control another individual, not even a little child, the more, perhaps, can we avoid feeling insulted. And this in turn would help us to get a bit less angry.

Knowing the Rules, Not Knowing How to Keep Them

Some people feel that the many transgressions which we encounter day in and day out, are due to the fact that the underfive does not have a properly developed conscience, that he does not know sufficiently right from wrong. On this basis they suggest that, when the child does wrong, we need to reinforce his conscience. We should remind him more forcefully and repetitively of what is right and wrong, and we should underscore it with something that will make it stick. Some advocate a deprivation or a punitive measure, or at least an enforced time for reflection such as, "Sit on this chair and think about it." These approaches may relieve the teacher's frustration and may allow her righteously to enjoy a little calm, but the child mostly responds by nursing his anger at the teacher instead of improving his conscience. As to any improvement in his behavior, it is usually limited to the times when he knows the teacher is watching.

How then can we best help the child? It is quite true that the preschooler's conscience is not fully developed and does not yet serve him effectively. We need to remind ourselves, however, that the main sources of the young child's standards and ideals are his parents. They, not the teacher, form the core of his conscience. The preschool teacher is, at best, an alternate or additional model who can somewhat extend the standards that the child acquires at home and help him to adapt them to the expectations of the nursery school setting. Where the nursery school teacher is most effective is in helping a youngster to make good use of what conscience he has and to handle his guilt properly. Thus, she can be very helpful indeed, by assisting the child to achieve the standards he already has and by teaching him to deal with situations in which he has disregarded the voice of his early conscience and let himself down.

Most transgressions are not caused by a lack of knowledge of right and wrong. In fact, whenever I have wanted to punish or discipline a child's misconduct I was usually pretty sure that he *did* know better, but still did the wrong thing. By contrast, when I feel a child really did not know the right thing to do, such as in a situation altogether new to him or one in which the school's rules are at odds with those of his parents, I do not feel he needs to be punished. I just calmly explain how he is expected to behave. I think what mostly makes things go wrong is the child's immature functioning: his immature ability to tolerate frustrations; his limited ability for judgment and foresight, to gauge time, to differentiate between what he thinks and what others think, what he does and what others will do, between pretend and real; and his inability to delay gratifications, to accept substitutions, to wait. These are the things that prevent the child from living up to his standards of right and wrong. He knows not to steal, but the cookies are too tempting to resist. For the nursery school teacher it is fortunate that we are usually dealing with such immaturities in personality functioning rather than with a total lack of conscience, because personality functioning is the area in which the nursery school teacher can most successfully help the child. This is what we are at school for, namely to help the child develop just these functions, to help him, in the broadest sense of the word, to adapt to reality and to himself, to within and to without, in as realistic a fashion as is possible for his age.

Reparation versus Punishment

What this means in practice is that when things have gone wrong, we have to help the child correct them. In the process of correcting them, we indirectly educate him as to the very qualities of perseverance, judgment, frustration tolerance, and reality testing which have failed him before. For a hundred different situations of wrong-doing there will be a hundred different, appropriate ways to correct them. It is much easier to follow the punitive course and to say, if a child does something wrong he is going to sit on a chair; or, if he does something wrong he is not going to have candy. But these are quick solutions, what I am suggesting is much more complicated. If a book is torn, the teacher has to gauge quickly whether this is the kind of child who could, with effort and help, Scotch tape a torn page. If there is spilled milk, is this the kind of child who would best wipe it up with a sponge, or with a mop? Could he manage even soap or a detergent to get the spot really clean, or would that seduce him into more messing? The teacher has to think out each situation and how to correct it effectively, and she must not let it rest until it is corrected as effectively as possible. I try my hardest in all situations to find something realistic that a child can do to make amends. When a child hurts another child, I find some way that he can help: he washes off the mud, or brings the Band-aid, or rubs on the soothing lotion I keep for these occasions, or, if none of these is possible, I suggest some special service of kindness to atone for the preceding cruelty. I do not insist the child say that he is sorry, because it is so often a phrase without feeling, and a service requires more effort and helps more toward soothing the victim's hurt feelings, if not his body.

Some people object that this approach is much too easy on the child. They feel, for example, that if a child steals another child's toy out of his locker he ought to be punished for that because stealing is a terrible thing. I feel that *returning* the stolen toy, and thereby making reparation, is the most important part. However, as a teacher, I am also concerned with helping the child recognize and utilize his conscience in an appropriate way. Instead of underscoring the moral side by retaliation or punitiveness, the process of reparation can be used to make the child aware of his guilty feelings and to show him how to handle them. Therefore I do not let it rest just with making up. I try to involve the child's knowledge of right and wrong by saying, "When we have done something wrong we feel bad. Making up will help you to feel better about it." He may reply, "Oh, I don't care. I don't feel bad." But I am not put off easily, so I add casually, "You say that now, but I know you would feel very bad about it later. I want to help you make up because this is the best way to manage it when one feels bad." By using the measure of reparation I work with two aims in mind: To develop those qualities in the personality which will help the child increasingly to achieve his own standards and, at the same time, to show him a way by which he can learn to deal effectively with guilty feelings. Why so much emphasis on dealing with guilty feelings? Simply because we know how poorly children usually deal with guilty feelings during the preschool years. When they feel bad, we know how often they provoke in order to get punished—"He's asking for it." In this way naughtiness piles upon naughtiness and a vicious cycle is created. Sometimes children who feel bad do not alert us to this at school but delay their provocations until they get home. They feel that the parent will surely disapprove of their misbehavior enough to punish them and thereby relieve them. This widens the circle of misbehavior and punishment. Soon the parents complain that their child has been much more naughty since he started school. These and other unfortunate ways of handling early guilt are due to the fact that young children cannot yet use it to anticipate inner anxiety and cannot refrain from wrongdoing. For this reason, I feel that the best we can do is to help them become aware of their guilty feelings and to make up for wrongdoings to alleviate them in a sensible manner.

I agree very much with people who say that this is a very difficult method to implement, that it is extremely difficult for the teacher, because in effect it ends up punishing her. Very often, indeed, the teacher is the one who has to put an enormous amount of time, thought, and energy into fitting the right reparation to the right situation at the right time. Very often it means that she has to come back to it at a time when she could be off duty. Sometimes she even needs to put in a few moments after school, when the mother comes to pick up the child and she has to say, "I'm sorry, Johnny cannot go home just yet. We still have to spend a few minutes on cleaning up the wall." It imposes great hardships, but I feel that it is work worth doing and an effort worth making because it belongs in the realm of nursery school education.

It is not easy on the children either. I recall a little boy who was in an endless cycle of doing something naughty and then feeling very bad about it, then doing something naughty again, and so on. Finally I said, "David, I am going to try to help you not to have to feel so bad all the time. I'll help you to make up for when you do things wrong." At first he was very relieved, but after a while, when we were once again working at picking up a pile of crayons and blocks which were scattered all over the room, he sat down and said, "Mrs. Furman, I think I will go back to feeling bad, it's more convenient." I know I am not proposing an easy way out either for the teacher or for the children. I hope it is a thoughtful way, but it is not one for which there is a ready prescription. When a teacher makes such an approach her own, she will have to give much time and energy to thinking out new situations every day with every child. This makes it difficult, but it is also fun—more challenging and more rewarding than the run-of-the-mill punishments.

Chapter 6

Living With Spiderman et al.— Mastering Aggression and Excitement

Ruth Hall

Why are they constantly playing the Incredible Hulk and Spiderman; how can we stop them from riling each other up with these TV characters; how can we get parents to turn off the TV; and what to do about those Underroos? These and similar questions reflect many teachers' concern and frustration with the extent to which the creatures of the TV screen dominate the play, and indeed the mental lives, of their young pupils. The preoccupation with superheroes which used to plague mainly the elementary school teacher now flourishes among the preschoolers. "In the old days," Superman and Batman were confined to comic books and, for the most part, were not available to children until they could read. But since the advent of television, the vivid antics of these and others portrayed in the cartoons are daily fare for children of all ages. Is television then the main culprit? Wouldn't it be nice if such a simple answer could be true! But earlier generations were equally concerned about such things as comic books, and the generations before that about pool-rooms, horse racing, and dancing. Every generation produces such entertainments and the young invariably find them fascinating. So the answer, of course, is that the causes do not lie in the current indulgences available. They lie rather in the eternal human condition, shaped by forces both inside and outside the child.

The task of the child as he grows is to learn to balance the urges from within against the stimulations and demands from without, so that he develops the capacity to do what he wishes to do, in ways that make him feel good, enhance his self-esteem, and enable him to adapt to his community. This task, throughout life, requires vigorous struggle and sometimes painful sacrifice. What are these forces?

FORCES FROM OUTSIDE THE CHILD

From the outside are the demands of the family that the child assume more and more responsibility for his own behavior. The child, from very early on, is keenly aware of the difference in size and skills between himself and the parents and longs to escape his own immaturity. Children do want to be big and to do as the loved adults do, but they do not always want to take the path the parents choose for them, nor do they want to achieve the kind of maturity their elders have in mind. Much of the time, very young children want to grow up instantly, without painstaking expenditure of effort on acquiring each skill in turn, without having to wait and practice and make mistakes, without having to accept limitations and compromises of any kind. Moreover, they often view the adults as "doing as they please" and as being powerful enough to control the world, and that's the way they want to be grown up. Adult demands, corrections, and restrictions are thus often not seen as a help toward getting big but as a frustrating reminder of being little and helpless. At best, such divergences of opinion bring about clashes in the parent–child relationship. It takes a lot of loving and understanding, as well as firmness and consistency, to assist children in taking over the parental values and standards and in using them effectively as a guide to behavior.

This thorny road is often made more difficult for parents and children by the advances in communication techniques which have brought about more widespread recognition of the many cultural differences among us. What is "right" for one group is "wrong" for another. Communities and neighborhoods used to be fairly self-contained and there was a general consensus among adults in a given area about what was right and what was wrong. Children as they grew could rely on "public opinion" enough to turn attention to personal opinion at a stage and rate that fit internal readiness. In today's world the choices regarding personal conduct are much broader and are introduced to very young children whether parents wish it or not. Everywhere we go we are bombarded with glamorized displays of sex and violence, not just on television, but in magazines, on the street corner, and in public parks. Any aberrant or extreme behavior can be loudly advocated by some group and the "right" to indulge publicly is demanded. This is seductive to children as it offers the choices of yielding to impulse, denying responsibility, and quick, easy solutions to problems. It also tempts parents to alter their expectations or to apply them inconsistently. Yet in such a cosmopolitan society, the parents and teachers of children need to be especially clear themselves in their beliefs and attitudes in order to have functional influence on the development of the young. For it is these close and beloved caretakers whom the children wish to emulate, and on whom they count for support in making choices and in building inner controls. Children take their cues from the behavior of those with whom they are intimate. If mom says, "Don't hit" but hits when angry, and presents cartoons as acceptable entertainment, her child will believe and live what she *does*, not what she says.

FORCES FROM INSIDE THE CHILD

The age of the child must be taken into account when discussing what comes from within. During the first year of life, the child is vulnerable to any big feeling. And any feeling the baby experiences can quickly become too big and result in overwhelming distress. The infant relies on mother, or the mothering person, to anticipate and ward off such events or to provide the calming influence which brings feelings back to a containable level. When mother is reliable in her sensitivity to her infant's emotional states, the child gradually develops an ever greater capacity for maintaining emotional balance. If she is not reliable, the infant experiences overwhelming states far too often. This can result in overstimulation of aggressive and excited tendencies which are not sufficiently contained by either child or mother and which are subsequently difficult to modulate and "tame." Sometimes circumstances beyond the mother's control, such as illness, the need for surgery, or unavoidable separations, can be felt by the child as lapses of reliability. These also overtax the infant's capacity to contain the feelings associated with primitive urges and bodily needs, and lead to the same difficulty in tolerating and mastering them.

As the child becomes mobile a new dimension is added. The child can now move away from mom in his play and often gets into trouble doing it. Mother now demands that he curb his impulses in the interests of safety. He may not pull things off the tables, or torment the cat, or eat food he finds on the floor. His mother gets upset over these things and says, "No, no!" A tough lesson must now be learned. In order to keep feeling loved and lovable he must give up the enormous pleasure of freely indulging these toddler impulses. The struggle to take in this fact of life is most vividly acted out around the issue of toilet mastery. Everyone knows of the "terrible twos" with its notorious tantrums and teasing. For a long time (at least if you are the mother, it seems so) the child attempts to have his cake and eat it too. For example, a mother with whom I work told me of finding her 20-month-old in the broom closet, smearing in the mess of a broken egg, saying over and over to himself, "No, no—no, no—no, no." He clearly showed his recognition, and indeed his beginning internalization of mother's wish concerning the egg, by hiding and saying "no, no" to himself, while simultaneously he enjoyed the lovely mess. The absurdity of such a compromise charms us all, and it is this quality in the toddler that keeps his caretakers as loving and as patient as he needs them to be. Only gradually and grudgingly does he bow to their civilizing intentions and accept them as a part of his own expectations of himself.

At times the child thoroughly enjoys his tug-of-war with mom but he does not always find the struggle fun, because when he feels anger it is still very intense. His rage consumes all his attention and energy and, for its duration, he cannot even remember or feel his love for the prohibiting adult. This is frightening indeed, and the "scary mad wishes" that Mr. Rogers talks about seem very dangerous. They stir up the worry of being unlovable and threaten the child with fears of abandonment. If mother can curb her frustrations and anger at the child's stressful behavior, his love for her wins out in the end.

With repeated experience the child comes to know that it is possible to be angry without endangering himself or his loved ones. He learns to modify his anger for the sake of his love, as mother does, and to take in her standards as his own. When the child begins to say no to himself and really to heed his own admonition, he feels safer in the world. He also feels better about himself as these first real achievements in becoming like the loved parents bring with them a new self-esteem: "I am a big boy (or girl) and I do it all by myself." Compliance with social requirements gets easier. This helps him take the next step away from mom toward independence. He is now ready for nursery school.

The preschooler has a new preoccupation. A keen pleasurable awareness develops regarding his or her body, especially its sexual feelings, characteristics, and functions. "Look at me," "See me," "Watch me" is the start of every sentence. It conveys the child's pleasure in showing off and in attracting admiration. Equally intent is his curiosity about others and need to compare himself with them. This inevitably confronts the child with the differences between the sexes and between the sexual attributes of children and adults. Thinking at this age is concrete and simplistic. More equals better, bigger equals better. If something is missing it is presumed lost, damaged, or stolen. If others are seen as more favorably endowed it rouses envy and anger and prompts wishes to exchange attributes, or to take away theirs, to spoil them or to appropriate them for oneself. All these thoughts make for a big worry about keeping intact. The age of the Band-aid has arrived and no household can have enough of them. It is a very big idea to ask of one so young to believe there can be two ways to be right, as boys and as girls. It is just as hard to accept that each will in time acquire the adult status of his or her own gender. The differences between the child's and adult's body are so great that it hardly seems possible to believe one could really change so much. The child is determined to discover the answer to his or her question about why people's bodies are so different, yet he or she often harbors terrifying ideas about what this answer might be. This is one reason for the young child's many questions about so many things, but rarely about the crucial differences between sexual attributes. Slowly children realize that these differences are all about the getting of babies, and a whole new set of wishes emerges.

During this time the child has not yet sorted out the possible from the impossible, feeling left out and inadequate is still very hard, and waiting to grow up seems like an eternity. His wishes, however, are very strong and magic happenings seem to occur daily. The child is therefore very vulnerable to the tempting example set by the magic people of television who can indulge their primitive urges and excitements, yet fend off any danger easily. If you had the power to fly or fight anyone you would not feel so small and never feel helpless. In addition, the big, angry thoughts of this age bring big, angry wishes to hurt loved family members. The preschooler tries not to have such mixed feelings and scary wishes, but for the most part succeeds only in steering them away from beloved people onto imaginary beasts, who then in retaliating anger plot to attack the child. This is the stuff of nightmares and monsters in the closet. Again the television provides such a feeling of reality to the monster ideas and stimulates the child's excited and angry fantasies that it is hard for little children to struggle against the fascination it exerts. They need adult intervention in order to demarcate better for themselves the line between the inner world of thoughts and feelings and the outside world of real events. Such increased self-awareness is an essential prerequisite toward gaining mastery and self-control. If mother can be in tune with the part of the child that wishes protection from the temptations, she will limit his TV viewing. She then usually finds that the child's protests are superficial and that the household is more peaceful once the rules are firm.

THE PARENTS' DILEMMA

One of the problems which makes this seemingly simple solution difficult is the wish on the part of parents not to limit themselves as the child is limited. The child sees older siblings and parents avidly watching fights, murders, magical doings, practical jokes, yelling, and insults, and he wishes to feel as they do instead of having his own confused reactions. It is hard for the young child to sort out what is real on television and what is not. Oscar the grouch is loved even though he behaves in nasty ways; the cookie monster eats even tables, chairs, and plates as well as cookies; an early morning news show has an actual rocket launch which is labeled real and in the afternoon a story show portrays a rocket launch which looks just as real but lands in the midst of grotesque creatures and guns that make people disappear. The T-shirt fad is a current example of a similar situation in which the parents' self-indulgence adversely affects their child. The parents think it is cute to dress a toddler in shirts with imprinted sayings which convey their mixed feelings about him ("Here comes trouble"; "Kid for rent") or imply sexual innuendos. The child is pleased, confused, ashamed, and embarrassed as people talk to him about the message on the shirt. Either he takes it as literally true and feels hurt, or he doesn't understand it at all, yet senses that the adults are excited by it. He wants to do as they do but finds himself excited, frightened, and humiliated all at once and ultimately feels alone, small, and exploited.

WHAT CAN BE DONE

As at the earlier ages, preschoolers too need their care-takers to help them clarify what upsets them and what comforts, so that the capacity to choose for themselves can grow. Self-control brings self-esteem, and self-esteem counteracts the overpowering feelings from inside. It is the only avenue to lasting mastery.

So now back to the original question, what to do about the youngsters' fascinated preoccupation with the imag-inary, ever-so-real characters of television. We need to accept the fact that these "problems" cannot be gotten rid of. Even if we could turn off all television and movies and prohibit the production and sale of Underroos, we would still be left with the same developmental issues and the challenging educational task of helping children to cope with them. The TV, the T-shirts, the toy guns, and all their equivalents do not create the children's excitement and aggression, or their wish for magical powers and effortless solutions. They merely stimulate, and some-times overstimulate these impulses, encourage infantile ways of dealing with them, and lend them a deceptive measure of pseudoreality and adult sanction. In doing so they attract, enhance, and gratify the part of the child's personality which is proportionately bigger and stronger and make it harder for the as yet immature and weaker parts to grow and to bring about inner balance and har-mony. When the child's mental forces are so uneven, he may look, and even feel as if he is having fun, but his behavior betrays lack of contentment, containment, and well-being. For example, the child who wears the Super-man suit may be unsafe with himself in trying to fly, or unsafe with others in trying to overpower them, or he may be unable to concentrate his attention and energy on learning and fail to acquire knowledge of the real world and skills to deal with it.

How can we help such children? A first step consists of intervening in the unsafe, or potentially unsafe behavior and of limiting the external sources of overstimulation, the TV programs, Superman suits, and toy weapons. But this is indeed only the first step. In the course of their daily play children then invent their own monsters and readily turn any random toy such as a block into a gun, reminding us that their feelings continue to surge up from within themselves. These feelings cannot be banished by prohibition, and it is better to address them as they arise. To some extent, pretend play is helpful. Fantasy is meant to give us a brief respite from harsh reality. However, when it is used to turn our backs on the real world altogether, it becomes an impediment to maturity. For the most part, therefore, feelings need to be coped with through mastery. This is a tall task, but one the child can accomplish when the excess stimulation and confusion from outside is diminished and when the educators support him in developing realistic and adaptive means of dealing with the inner and outer world.

These means are the same for all developmental struggles. The most important is the use of words. Through words teachers can help children *and* parents to understand the wish to be big, the wish for and fear of magical solutions, the struggle over excited and angry feelings, the reality of what can and cannot happen, and how important it is for the loved adults to uphold this reality. As children learn to use words as a substitute for action and as a means of clarifying, tolerating, and containing feelings, they gradually gain self-control. The straightest road to taming the classroom monsters and superhuman beings leads through self-control to inner safety and self-esteem. A confident and competent child has less need for magic.

Chapter 7

Learning to Feel Good About Sexual Differences

Erna Furman

Along with much other growing and learning, the preschooler, roughly between the ages of 3 and 5 years, has to accomplish an important developmental task: to know and accept one's own sexual identity as a boy or girl, to know what one will grow up to be, and what one's sexual role is as man or woman, to understand and accept, even like, sexual differences, and to tolerate one's immature sexual status. The children's interest in this whole topic receives its impetus from maturational forces which intensify their sexual sensations during this period and heighten their sensitivity to manifestations of sexuality in others.

Since the children's feeling and thinking about sexual matters unfolds within the setting of the immediate family, their relationships and experiences with the closest loved ones play the most important part. And thus, although young boys or girls may grapple with this developmental task largely within the silence of their own minds and hearts, parents usually have an opportunity to recognize some of their child's concerns and to assist

101

him or her in sorting them out. In the nursery school or
day care center, by contrast, we see very few direct signs
of the preschoolers' sexual feelings, questions, and behavior. What we do see are the many ways in which the
children's attempts to deal with their sexual concerns
interweave with and affect other areas of their personality functioning. This enables us to gauge, to some extent, whether a child is addressing this phase-appropriate
task and struggling with it more or less successfully and
it enables us also to help him or her in different ways.
Let us therefore take a closer look at some of these manifestations and how we might deal with them to further
the children's emotional growth.

BEHAVIORS AFFECTED BY SEXUAL INTERESTS
AND CONCERNS AND HOW TEACHERS HELP

At entry to nursery school a child's main age-appropriate concern is, "How will I measure up?" "Will they
think me big, strong, smart, handsome, or pretty?" Sometimes these questions are asked in words, more often they
(and the children's own answers to them) are reflected in
their behavior. Some children indicate this by being a bit
shy and hesitant in their approach to the teacher, peers,
and materials, others hide it behind a little showing off
to impress us with words or deeds, or, "I can climb that
slide. I am used to an even bigger one at my Grandma's,"
or, "At my house we have harder puzzles!" The mere fact
that such feelings about adequacy and comparison with
others are present, already shows us that the child has
begun to grapple with these developmental concerns, but
we learn more about how he or she is coping with them
by observing how they affect the daily behavior. A little
shyness or bravado, soon overcome, suggests a sufficient
amount of overall self-esteem with adequate resources to

work at proving oneself through realistic accomplishments. Some youngsters, however, encounter more difficulty. Their shyness is extreme and persistent and interferes with their efforts and success in mastering skills and activities. Or they need to compensate for feelings of inadequacy by noisily intimidating or belittling others, by repeatedly displaying their "superiority" over them, by dressing up in fancy party clothes and jewelry or in cowboy outfits and Superman shirts, carrying toy weapons or other status symbols and bringing many impressive, though not necessarily appropriate things to show. And others yet use mother as a protective shield against presumed inferiority and as a source of self-esteem. This is a most common factor in cases of prolonged separation difficulty. As long as mother is present the child relies on her good opinion and support of him and he does not have to face feeling judged on his own merit; as one little girl said when, after weeks of clinging to mother, she finally prepared herself for entering the school on her own, "But Mommy, they will all laugh at me when I'm on my own."

Many teachers sense such children's underlying concern and know to help them. They make a point of appreciating the child's positives. They sympathize in words how hard it is to be new because one isn't so sure people will really like one. Above all, they assist the child in finding activities that they can learn to do well and which will enable them to feel competent and proud of their achievements. Nothing helps self-esteem as much as real accomplishment that has been achieved through hard work.

Of course, the wish to look well and do well, to show off and gain admiration, remains the preschooler's main theme in life, and nursery school teachers are used to the constant tune of, "Look at me." They do not as such dis-

courage it but they guide it. Whereas many youngsters
would show off anything, from bare chests and bottoms
to Grandpa's latest gift of a "He-Man" toy, teachers make
it clear that, most of all, they value and praise persistent
effort, learning, and realistic achievement in knowledge,
skills, self-control, and appropriate behavior. They tell
the child who merely pulls up his shirt and flexes his
muscles for admiration that at school people want to admire what work those muscles can do and offer, for example, to practice throwing and catching a ball with him
so he will really have something to show. They notice
that another child always wants to be looked at in yet
another new outfit in the housekeeping corner, perhaps
because he is afraid to try his hand at an activity that
requires effort, and they tell him that it's time to work
at blocks or art projects, that something one makes, however humble, is always worth more than something one
just puts on. They spot the child who always paints the
same picture and, instead of admiring it yet another time,
encourage him to try a new idea, technique, or color combination to really earn their compliment. And they are
not put off by the child who will not ever draw because
he "doesn't like to," but expect him or her to spend a little
time doing just that, because they suspect that such an
avoidance may mean, "I don't know how to and I won't
be good at it"; and they are then especially supportive
and appreciative of his beginning attempts. Also, teachers help children not merely to seek and rely on the admiration of others, but to appraise their own performance
and to do so realistically, neither belittling nor exaggerating their achievements, for they know that being right-
fully pleased with themselves builds children's confidence
and self-esteem more effectively than outside recognition
alone. In fact, some youngsters offer up their picture for
praise without even looking at it themselves, but when

the teacher asks for their self-appraisal first, she finds that they really did not think much of it. That provides an opportunity for helping the child to appreciate his work more or, if it really is not good enough, to encourage him to try again and improve it. Another child, of course, may vastly overestimate his productions, may need help to acknowledge its shortcomings and to correct them.

Ongoing comparison and competition with others usually accompanies the wish to be best and the worry about being less or least good. Many youngsters try to climb the top rung of the ladder, literally and figuratively, by putting down others in word or even deed. The refrain of, "I can do it better," and "You don't even know how to" is often oblivious to the feelings of others, just as it may be out of line with the boaster's own real accomplishments. Here teachers have a chance to help with consideration and tolerance as well as respect for differences between people. They assist children in becoming aware of each other's feelings and praise and admire the one who can tone down his anger and show kindness or even help a buddy with a skill or task. Teachers often talk about people finding some things harder or easier than others, about being good at different things without being a better or worse person, about having had more or less occasion to learn or practice something without being "dumb" or a "baby." They stress that we can admire others and learn from them without feeling inferior and that each can feel good about him or herself when we make sure we are doing our best and can improve on our own past performance. Jeremy, who has long since learned to put on his boots, can feel proud for working well at his hard zipper and Justin can feel proud for learning to manage his boots, which is very hard for him, but Jane can not rest on her laurels of having mastered boots and zipper and use them to lord it over the others. She needs to tackle her next job which perhaps is tying laces. Moreover, whereas Jane is currently better at dressing skills, Jeremy may be ahead in climbing and jumping and Justin may be especially good at singing, and they can all learn some things from and respect each other.

Intense curiosity about others is part and parcel of the preschooler's developmental interests and pleasures. Since as teachers we often find every detail of our appearance scrutinized and our private lives insistently questioned, most of us can readily appreciate that our young pupils' inquisitiveness focuses on personal intimate matters—"You got a new pin, Mrs. Smith. It's nice. Who gave it to you?" "Do you have a Daddy at home?" "Do you sleep with him in the same bed?" "Why don't you have any children? When will you?" "You have a fancy dress today. Where are you going after school?" And when we introduce our charges to animals or take them to the zoo, their observations and questions relate even more out-spokenly to bodily functions and sexual characteristics —"Look, this one is the Daddy!" "Look how much peepee he can do!" Although teachers respond to most of these comments with matter-of-fact clarifications, their main task is to channel the children's lively curiosity into learning about the less personal world around us and to help them use their growing powers of observation and reasoning to figure out how it works. Thus the preschool-ers' endless "whys" and "hows," rooted in their puzzle-ments about the sexual differences and roles, are assisted, step by step, to branch out and encompass nonbodily things and events. It is a slow process. Initially, young children's thinking is so closely linked to their personal feelings and bodily experiences that they conceive the external nonpersonal world in those same terms. The steam shovel "eats" the dirt, the wrecking crane "bashes up the house" as if in a violent ill-temper. An incident, reported by a preschool teacher, illustrates particularly well a boy's transitional step from body to machine. The children were grinding carrots, using a hand-operated old-fashioned meat grinder. At his request, the teacher then helped him to take the grinder apart, inspect each section, and put it together again. He concentrated so calmly and intently on the task and seemed to grasp so well how each part contributed to making the grinder work, that the teacher thought his interest and understanding were already distanced from the body-related framework. She learned otherwise. When, after assembling the grinder, only the wingscrew was left, the boy asked where it went. "In front here, where the ground pieces come out." "Oh, that's not the front," said he, "that's the back. Don't you know that all the food always comes out at the back?" The teacher could then explain that machines and bodies worked differently in some ways, helping her pupil to take a big new step in comprehension.

The preschoolers' body-focused feeling and thinking and especially their puzzlements and misgivings about sexual differences often manifest themselves in concerns about the integrity of body parts and the dangers of potential injury. We hear many comments and questions to that effect. Four-year-old Lisa asked whether Jewish boys' skullcaps can come off; her contemporary, Brian, on seeing a bandage around Susan's wrist, wondered whether her hand had fallen off; haircuts are anathema to many little boys; and when Anne wore a leg cast to correct a minor orthopedic problem, several of her nursery school peers thought her leg had been taken off, although the procedure and the reasons for it had been explained to them beforehand. Most commonly the children's concerns surface in undue worry about their own minor scratches and bruises and in frequent demands for Band-Aids which may be applied to injuries so tiny that only they can "see" them. Some youngsters, especially boys, are so scared that they need to deny potential danger or hurt altogether, frightening us instead with their heedless daredevil behavior and provocative disregard for safety rules. Teachers do of course show appropriate sympathy with even little hurts and do enforce safety measures firmly, but they also help in other ways. They stress that taking good, sensible care of oneself is a mark of growing up and becoming self-reliant and independent. It includes finding out about and understanding hazards realistically and acting accordingly, being neither reckless nor unduly fearful—be this gauging the weather conditions to choose appropriate clothes and learning how to put them on, or mastering safe ways of handling toys and tools, or being knowledgeable about one's bodily skills so that one may reasonably estimate whether one can or cannot make a certain jump. It also includes using pain sensibly as an inner guide and warning signal. If we either deny or exaggerate pain, or are unable to tell the difference between small, medium, and big hurts, we cannot take proper care of ourselves or ask for the right help. In short, teachers show that they value realistic assessment and self-care and are eager to help the children achieve them.

Young children's concerns about differences are particularly pronounced in their encounters with people whose appearance or behavior in some, sometimes quite minor, way deviates from their familiar norm. Unless the caring adults are tuned into the youngsters' hypersensitivity, can take the lead in verbally acknowledging the unusual, and welcome the children's ideas and questions, they may remain quite unaware of just how keenly such differences are observed and frequently misjudged. In one nursery school a newcomer had a missing finger on one hand. It was a congenital anomaly which in no way affected the boy's dexterity and which indeed went unnoticed by many adults. Since no adult had discussed it, the children did not say anything about it either, but in time there were subtle repercussions. One boy repeatedly refused to sit next to the afflicted child, another began to avoid using his hands in small muscle activities, and one girl suddenly complained about not liking school. In exploring the causes of these children's difficulties it turned out that they were related to their hitherto unvoiced worries about the newcomer's handicap. When the teacher then finally discussed it with everyone, it became clear that all the children had noticed the missing finger and had questions about how and why it had happened, could it happen to them and was it perhaps "catching." We know now that children observe and question not only anomalies or handicaps or signs of injury but also other differences which appear strange to them. This includes unfamiliar racial or ethnic features of body, clothes, speech, or manners; it includes changes in the appearance of familiar people, such as a new haircut, pregnancy, a wig or other features of dress or makeup; and it includes behaviors stemming from bodily or emotional difficulties, such as spasticity, tantrums, crying spells, hyperactivity, and many others. Whenever possible, teachers help children by preparing them ahead for such encounters, by explaining the reasons for the unfamiliar, by welcoming and answering children's comments about them, and even by alerting their parents so that they will be able to understand and deal with their children's questions and responses at home. Teachers further help by supporting their pupils' capacity for accurate observation, however touchy the topic may be, because they know how important it is that this faculty stand them in good stead (how can they later learn to distinguish a "b" from a "d" if they are expected to be oblivious to minor differences?), and they assist them in delineating and understanding the nature of whatever difference they observe: for example, they point out that a difference in ethnic or racial traits is limited to just that and does not imply differences in feelings, aptitudes, or other bodily or mental characteristics, or, that, similarly, a specific bodily or mental handicap may interfere with a person's functioning in certain areas but does not affect them in others, that they enjoy the same things, feel the same pains, and can do or learn the same activities as everyone else.

How does all this relate to helping preschoolers with concerns about sexual identity and differences? When we help children with their thinking, feeling, and understanding in these other areas, every step in mastering them strengthens their ability to come to grips with the sexual aspects of their development. For example, liking oneself as a boy or girl is furthered by self-esteem in general, by being relatively independent in bodily self-care, by being able to work at and achieve well in age-appropriate skills and activities, in short, by feeling that one is a worthwhile competent "somebody." At the same time, helping children understand and master other areas also enables them to differentiate sexual concerns from other aspects of their own and other people's functioning. For example, a boy's or girl's struggle with understanding the nature and adequacy of their sexual identity and immaturity may distort their attitude to injuries and handicaps or to ethnic and racial differences between people. When they gain a realistic appreciation of such matters, they can keep their sexual concerns within proper perspective, prevent them from encroaching inappropriately on other domains, and thus make them more manageable just because they remain limited to their own sphere. These ways of helping children, albeit indirect, contribute so importantly to their chances of successfully mastering developmental sexual concerns, that they indeed constitute not only the teachers' but even the parents' most effective educational tools. No amount of sexual enlightenment or reassurance can help children to feel good about themselves unless it is accompanied by and takes place in the context of learning to be realistic, competent, and considerate.

DEVELOPMENTAL SEXUAL BEHAVIOR IN THE NURSERY SCHOOL AND HOW TEACHERS HELP

Young children's thinking about sexual roles and differences is closely tied to their sexual feelings and impulses, which maturationally arise within their own bodies and minds, which are exciting and pleasurable and which they seek to gratify in real or imagined interactions with their loved ones. It is impossible for preschoolers to separate intellectual understanding either from instinctual excitement or from their loving relationships. Every experience in one of these areas inevitably touches off the others. When intellect, excitement, and loving relationships are sufficiently balanced, they interact helpfully and the child's personality can contain and master them. However, this inner balance is always precarious and young children's means of coping with stimuli, from within and without, are very limited. Their impulses and feelings easily outstrip their means of mastery, overpower their personality, rule their behavior, and become a source of concern to themselves and others. It is hard enough for in-tune parents to gauge the ups and downs of their child's inner struggles within the context of the family relationship and to assist him or her in maintaining a manageable equilibrium, be it by offering helpful intellectual clarifications at appropriate times, or by limiting sources of external stimulation, or by expecting the child to curb his or her excited gratification-seeking behavior with them and others. The parents' and child's task is made much harder when outsiders who, however well liked, are after all not the child's primary loved ones, interfere, either stimulate and gratify the child's excitement, or attempt to take over the parental role of guiding the child's sexual development. Parents and children usually sense that these matters are private family business and nursery schools and day care centers help them best by supporting this approach. They keep the children's bodily interactions with peers and adults to a minimum and provide a setting in which the youngsters' more neutral noninstinctual growth and learning are fostered, where they are introduced to the behavioral norms of the wider community, and helped to distinguish its rules, expectations, and satisfactions from those of the home.

Specifically, preschool teachers limit bodily affection, such as kissing, hugging, and lapsitting and promote shared pleasures in verbal exchanges and joint activities; they encourage self-care in dressing, washing, eating, and toileting as well as privacy in bathrooms, with the help of doors or curtains, and at naptimes, by using portable screens and allowing children to remain dressed; they do not plan sessions on sex education and do not provide equipment designed to introduce sexual topics, such as "sex dolls"; they discourage games with excessive body contact, such as the use of peers in acting out doctor games, undressing and lying down together in playing family, or free-for-all wrestling and roughhousing; they limit indulgence in exciting fantasy pursuits, keep birthday and holiday celebrations low key, interfere with games and activities involving high-pitched excitement, and do not allow swearing or the use of sexual words for purposes of enticement or humiliation. The use of such measures reflects the preschool's respect for the children's meager means of coping with stimulation, assists youngsters in focusing their energies on learning and working and enjoying their achievements and on interacting happily with others in a calmer, more considerate manner. It also indirectly diminishes the incidence of sexual behavior. Whenever, in my work with preschools, the teachers justifiably complained of a widespread lack of concentration, of a prevalence of excited-aggressive peer play, of a general "high pitch" and repeated sexual play among the children, we could trace the immediate sources of overstimulation within the setting and correct them readily. In several day care centers the mere introduction of bathroom and naptime privacy produced a marked change for the better.

A helpful preschool atmosphere also provides the best setting for teachers to assist youngsters when they do show their developmental sexual interests and concerns and for the children to utilize their guidance. The following are among the most common sexual manifestations: children may ask questions or make comments about sexual matters, sometimes revealing their misunderstandings or confusion. They may masturbate in various forms, such as touching their genitals or behinds, pressing their thighs together, or wiggling on seats. They may curiously peek or stare at the bodies of others, often in connection with toileting, or exhibit their own nudity, sometimes leaving the bathroom without pulling up their pants. They may, perhaps under the guise of doctor or family play, handle another child's body or allow themselves to be handled, or may join with a partner in the excited use of dolls to act out sexual fantasies. How does the teacher respond? With verbal sexual questions and comments she usually replies briefly or points out that there is a "mixup." With masturbatory activities, the teacher suggests quietly that such things are not done in front of others and offers the child the choice of either stopping or removing himself to the privacy of a bathroom stall. With curiosity and exhibitionism in action, the need for each person's privacy is stressed and enforced. With sexual interactions with a partner, the children are expected to stop and are given the reasons that bodies are private and that doing such things together becomes too exciting which, in the end, turns fun into feeling bad and out of control. It is of course helpful when the adult remains calm and matter-of-fact and does not respond emotionally with shock, upset, anger, or knowing smiles. First-time occurrences are thus essentially used to spell out the school rules on respect for the privacy (not secrecy!) of one's own and others' bodies and sexual feelings. This, plus perhaps a second-occasion reminder, suffices for most children who are still learning how to contain their sexual feelings socially and are not burdened by marked inner concerns.

Teachers are wise, however, also to tell the child that they will let Mommy know about their conversation so that she can give further answers or clear up misunderstandings or, if there was some sexual behavior, that they will tell her what happened so that she can help in case there are some questions or worries about bodies or body parts. If there is opportunity for a private talk at pick-up time, teacher and child may inform the mother together and repeat to her the reasons for sharing the incident, or the teacher may need to arrange to phone the parent later in the day. In taking this step, the teacher helps the children understand that she not only wants to assist them in learning socially accepted rules of sexual privacy—which by law all of us have to follow outside the home—but also wants to pave the way for children to address their sexual feelings and concerns with the parents who can understand and help best.

Their children's sexual feelings and concerns are usually a sensitive topic for parents. Even so, when teachers share such information with the parent thoughtfully and calmly and convey their respect for the parental role in these matters, many parents are appreciative and able to help their children. However, there are also many who react with embarrassment and guilt, feeling that their child committed an indiscretion which reflects poorly on their parenting. Moreover, many parents feel at a loss as to how to handle sexual concerns with their children. Their distress and quandary may then show in being critical and angry with the child or in blaming the school and other children for "teaching him bad habits," or they may ask the teacher to talk about it all with the child, handing over their parental prerogative and responsibility. Many of us who have not had the benefit of help with sexual matters from our own parents, find it very difficult to handle them with our children. The alert teacher senses the parent's discomfort, whatever form it may take, and suggests that they set up a parent–teacher conference to talk things over. At that time she assures the parent that her mention of the incident implied neither criticism of the parent or child nor a serious concern about the child. Rather, she assumed that the child, like all youngsters, was trying to cope with age-appropriate developmental interests and felt that the parents, who care so much about all aspects of their child's growth, have the right to be kept informed and may find it helpful to know. Through their long-standing intimate knowledge of their child's feelings and experiences they can best evaluate such an isolated piece of behavior and help him or her, if they feel it is indicated. The teacher does not accept a parent's request to take over their task with the child, but may offer to help them understand and even talk with the child. She stresses that (1) sexual matters are best addressed within the framework of the parent–child relationship, not only because children feel so uniquely close and loyal to their parents, but because it helps children to appreciate that sexuality belongs with the closest, most important loving relationships, and (2) parents need not be perfect at handling this or any other educational aspect. Some parents even tell their children that they unfortunately find it hard to deal with sexual matters and may make mistakes in talking about them which they will then try to correct, but they do want to help them sort things out and feel comfortable about them. Children benefit more from their parents' halting efforts and good will than from the expertise of an outsider to the family. If the teacher can support parents and listen well, they can usually figure out whether something is bothering the child and what it may be, and the teacher can then contribute some suggestions on wording clarifications or instituting helpful educational measures. Of course, some parents may not agree with her ideas, or may not want help from a teacher or from anyone else. The final say is theirs. The teacher can only assure them that she will be available for further discussion at a later time of their choosing. It is surprising how many parents do return for a talk after some thought and how many more, without necessarily letting the teacher know, are helped by her thoughtful and respectful attitude—perhaps to become just as thoughtful and respectful with their child, to think and feel with him and even help him or her themselves, or to seek advice elsewhere.

SYMPTOMATIC SEXUAL BEHAVIOR AND HOW TEACHERS HELP

Sometimes the child's questions, confusions, and/or above-mentioned behavioral manifestations persist, become repetitive, and even interfere with his or her learning and school adjustment. For example, a child may not be able to use his hands for activities because they are constantly engaged in touching his genitals, or cannot become interested in using the available toys and materials because he cannot relinquish a stereotyped doctor play, or cannot interact with peers without engaging in bodily excitement with them, or cannot use the bathroom without showing his nudity or sexual curiosity, or cannot learn and converse about other topics because of a pressing preoccupation with sexual questions. Sometimes, too, children seem driven to entice or follow others in semi-clandestine sexual play involving either mutual looking and touching or suggestive of sexual intercourse or other sexual practices.

All such instances constitute an "SOS," an indication that the child cannot cope with inner turmoil and is desperately calling for help. This is true even when children look like they are having "fun," when they apparently try to conceal their words and actions from the adults or deny what they said or did when confronted.

Teachers help by pointing out that the child is showing a trouble (not a naughtiness!), that such a trouble is not really fun but comes from worries. Right now these worries seem to boss the child, instead of the child being boss of them, and it will be important to tell Mommy about it so she can help by understanding what is bothering so much. In the meantime, though, the teacher will help at school by making rules that will at least help those troubles not to get worse and will also protect the other children, because a teacher's job is to keep everyone safe and comfortable. Depending on the nature of the difficulty, such rules may include a structured plan of activities, prohibition of associating with certain peers, using the bathroom only with adult supervision, and many more.

Usually, when such troubled children feel that the
teacher is sympathetic and helpful rather than punitive,
they, or at least a part of them, want to cooperate as best
they can.

In these situations, setting up a parent–teacher conference is not just wise but mandatory. Now there really
is a concern about the child's healthy development. The
parents will inevitably be more touchy and the teacher's
task is more difficult. Tact and calm, as opposed to alarm
and criticism, do nevertheless help to convey appropriate
concern and to enlist the parents in seeking a constructive
approach. In some instances the parents may be able to
pinpoint the source of the problem and, with the teacher's
support, help their child; in others it may be necessary
to assist the parents in obtaining professional advice. The
cause, or causes, of children's sexual concerns are quite
varied. Though excessive stimulation by the environment, in one form or another, generally plays a part,
actual seductions or molestations are not necessarily involved.

There are yet other situations a teacher needs to watch
out for, assess, and discuss with the parents, and that is
when an older preschooler manifests neither direct nor
indirect signs of phase-appropriate interests: there are no
verbal sexual references and no sexual behavior or excitement and, more importantly, no phase-appropriate
"Look at me!," "Look at what I have (know, can do)," no
interest in competing with others, no observing of and
responding to changes and differences in people's ap-
pearances or actions, and no curiosity to learn about the
world. Such a lack suggests that the child is not addressing his or her developmental tasks. This may be due to
restriction or inhibition if the general impression is one
of avoidance or withdrawal from all such activities, or it
may indicate a lag in development, if toddlerlike mani-

festations, such as teasing, messing, and possessive controlling, are prominent in lieu of more advanced concerns and satisfaction. The teacher, as always, helps by encouraging age-appropriate behavior and interests, but she also shares her observation with the parents. Sometimes they observe much more phase-appropriate manifestations at home and then the question to be addressed is what interferes with the child's functioning at the school or center. In other instances, the child's behavior is not different at home but the parents may have been unaware that this points to a concern. We sometimes find the behavioral signs of a child's emotional growing pains difficult to live with and so it helps to remind ourselves that even the strains and stresses of growing are preferable to a standstill in development.

WHAT ABOUT HOMOSEXUALITY IN PRESCHOOLERS?

This is often a special concern of teachers and parents and is mostly voiced in regard to boys when they show feminine behavior, such as in mannerisms and gait, or in their way of talking, or in dressing up and taking girls' or women's parts in play. Actually, girls manifest masculine behavior just as often, but this does not distress the adults in the same way. It is important to keep in mind that all young boys and girls occasionally wish they were of the opposite sex and periodically do take that role in play or behavior. This is part and parcel of their coming to terms with their own sexual identity as well as of feeling out what others are about so as to understand them better. In some ways it is similar to when children briefly experiment with, for example, being blind by walking around with their eyes closed, after encountering a blind person. To put themselves in another's shoes literally, helps them to feel with him or her.

We need to be concerned only when a child's preference for belonging to the opposite sex is persistent and exclusive, in the sense that he or she dislikes or avoids their own sexual identity in word and/or action. Even then such an attitude does not constitute homosexual or transsexual behavior nor does it presage such an outcome in later life. Young children are in the midst of learning to accept and like their own sexual identity and future role as well as that of others, and the eventual outcome of their developmental struggles cannot yet be determined. The persistent nonacceptance of his or her own identity at this early stage is of concern, however, for another reason. It points to children not feeling good about themselves as they are. When one wants to be someone else, it is not so much because the other seems so desirable but because one does not enjoy, or even feels endangered, being oneself.

Teachers therefore help, not by distracting, persuading, or disgracing the child, nor by removing the "props" and forbidding the unwelcome behavior, but by focusing on the core of the trouble and by helping parents to do likewise, "I'm so sorry you don't want to be yourself. Why do you not like yourself? What's wrong with being Jimmy (or Jane)?" With this, as with other sexual matters, the teacher's task is to gauge whether and when there is cause for concern, to set the tone for approaching it, to share her observations and handling with the parents, and to support their understanding of and assistance to their child. When parents listen sympathetically, children often can and do reveal what makes them feel wrong, inadequate, unattractive, unlovable, or unsafe, and parents can then help them to clear up misunderstandings or to correct some situations. Sometimes the teacher can assist parents in their task, sometimes she needs to help them seek out an appropriate professional person.

ON SEXISM

Teachers and parents, especially mothers, sense that the preschoolers' relative success or failure in coping with sexual identity and differences lays the foundation for later sexual attitudes. Concerned with sexism in the adult community, they are therefore particularly eager to influence the youngsters' development in this respect. The question is how best to go about it and, specifically, how can teachers help boys and girls to value and respect their own and others' sexuality and build mutually considerate relationships which appropriately include the sexual aspects.

We have already discussed the most important ways in which preschool teachers contribute: they support the growth of realistic self-esteem and help children understand and tolerate differences of all kinds among people, without either minimizing or exaggerating their effect on the whole person. They assist children in coming to terms with their sexual concerns by avoiding overstimulation, by assessing each child's ability to deal with this developmental task as it manifests itself in the preschool settings, and by assisting them and their parents in resolving potential or existing difficulties in the context of their intimate family relationships.

Beyond that, teachers help by setting the example of their own overall attitude of respect and appreciation for both sexes, young and old, and by conveying in word and behavior that "it takes both" to make the world go 'round. The significance of expending effort on using terms like *mailperson* or on insisting that everyone has to do the same activities to prove their equality as persons, pales in comparison to the meaningful impact of a thoughtful, rather than defensive, atmosphere of realistic respect.

Part II

Chapter 8

Helping Children with Speech

Ruth Hall

I have had a long-term interest in effective communication that grew out of my early work as a speech pathologist I will begin by describing a child that I knew before I began my training in child psychotherapy. She was a 5-year-old girl who had come to the agency I worked for because no one had been able to understand why she did not talk or learn well. She was clearly not a retarded child, she was physically capable, and she had a twin sister who functioned normally. She just didn't fit any category. We were to attempt to sort out what could be interfering with her growing up. I worked with her for the better part of a year, enjoying her and she me, but getting very little result. She would obediently imitate words, but she never used them for communication.

After an interruption for spring break, upon our return she came into the room and astonished me by going to the blackboard, picking up the chalk, and writing, *in script*, "I love you." Clearly, language was not a problem for the child. It was intact, indeed precocious, but it was not functional. There were things I just did not know at that time about how to make language become a functional skill for her. The experience helped start me on my path to further training. I have looked back with regret since, because I feel that child taught me more than I taught her.

In this discussion I will describe the path of speech development, when it begins, the route it takes, how it gets off the track, and what we as parents, teachers, and therapists can do to help.

THE EARLY MOTHER–CHILD DIALOGUE

Speech does not begin at the age of 1 or 2, when the child starts saying words. It begins long before that at the very moment mother and child first make contact with one another. Klaus and Kennell (1976) have described it beautifully when they talk about the bonding moment in the very first interaction between mother and child. The mutual gazing that goes on between mother and newborn baby is so gratifying, it brings a feeling that both mother and baby seek to repeat over and over. This sets in motion *all* forms of development, but speech in particular. As the baby and mother look at one another and share their joy together, a feeling of mutual understanding occurs. In the weeks that follow, baby begins to make noises and mother is so delighted she makes noises back. One of the most gratifying things I can recall was my utter surprise and delight when I discovered that my own baby really did say "goo." Of course I "gooed" right back, as happens with everyone. It is virtually impossible for any adult to pick up a baby and not make baby noises, to chatter and goo, and gurgle, and the baby grins and does it too. Everyone feels good, everyone is happy about it. The more the mother does it the more the baby does it. It makes for very good feelings and gets the use of verbal interaction off the ground. As the baby grows and the rituals of daily life progress, this still wordless dialogue continues, but mother begins to name things. Everything she touches, everything she does, every move she makes, she accompanies with talk. The baby babbles along and enjoys her talk, which to the baby is like music that goes along with daily happenings in the bath, at bedtime, with stories, and with eating. As the baby and mother go through the routines of the day, which are repeated over and over throughout each day and each week and each month, baby begins to know that when he makes noise, mom listens. Mom listens and responds. Sound begins to have a magical, powerful quality. The first year is the time when everything about the mouth feels good. It is the avenue for food and for talking. The baby is very much in tune with this part of his body and loves the sound and feel of making noises. At 6–7 months of age the mother often wakes in the morning to hear the baby babbling, cooing, gurgling to himself, quite content enjoying playing with sounds—for a few minutes—until he decides he misses her. Then the noise is not so pleasant, but still it is a noise that calls mom and she comes.

At the end of the first year it becomes clear that the baby is really understanding much of what mother says. When she says, "Do you want a cookie?" he looks at the cookie box. When she says, "Do you want to go bye-bye?" he reaches for his hat. He clearly knows her words, not just from the routine, but he knows what she is saying. The expansion and development of what he knows and what she knows he knows continues throughout the last part of that first year, and soon baby begins to say words back. These first words—one word can contain a whole sentence—are so valued, so delighted in by both the mother and the child that each word is treated like a gift and the pleasure that it brings makes the child want to say more. The more he talks the more he wants to talk, and the more he talks the more magic the words seem to bring.

I'd like to describe here a little boy for whom this did not work. The anecdote illustrates how important it is, when the child first starts saying those ill-pronounced words of the 1-year-old, that mother hear the words as words that actually say something. I had occasion to know this little boy from the time he was born, because I was working with his older brother who also had speech difficulties. The second child, to his mother's surprise and delight, went through his whole first year babbling, enjoying sounds, and talking to her, not with words, but with feelings and with noises, and she talked back in the very ordinary, delightful fashion. She was astonished each time she heard him in the morning at his babbling sound play. She was delighted by it. But somehow when he got to that one-year level, as he started with beginning words of *ma, da, bye-bye*, she could not hear them as words. She wanted them to be words, but since they were not clearly spoken, she could not accept these first attempts as real words. She would say, "But he doesn't say anything yet. Why doesn't he say anything?" Her worry that he did not talk became great. His attempts continued; I could hear them, others could hear them, but his mother could not. The attempts did not improve in their intelligibility and did not expand. He was almost 2½ before the mother could hear the attempts he made as true speech and during that 1½ years many other things in the child's development got off track. He was not able to feel understood, he was not able to make her know what he wanted without gestures, without acting things out, or showing her. He became a very hyperactive, very busy little fellow who needed to be watched every second. He really was not safe and she was not able to toilet train him. They were stuck on this one step of communication that was very frustrating to the boy and set him in paths that were difficult to overcome. By 2½, mother began hearing his efforts at communication and it began to expand. By age 5 he entered a preschool program, doing quite well. His speech is adequate now and very intelligible. He still has some minor difficulties with impulse control. He is on the active side but can be managed and has only occasional lapses in his toilet training. The difficulties in all these areas relate very much to the difficulty which began in the first part of the second year. This is very typical of one way that things get off track when communication is ineffective.

During that second year many things begin to happen with speech. In the normal course of events, if the mother is hearing the child's words, his vocabulary begins to expand and develop. It is a time when the child takes great pleasure in talking, in saying words, in naming things, in demanding and asserting himself with words. It is also a time of great fun between mother and child when they play with nursery rhymes and verses and jingles. This good feeling helps to offset the distress he feels that belongs to the developmental phase which is going on. During this age the child experiences the rise of ambivalence. "Shall I pull the doggie's hair or shall I pet him?" "Shall I use the pot or shall I *not* use the pot?" This is a big and a hard struggle. The good times that mom and baby can have playing with sounds, feeling they can understand one another in their communications, and in mom's acceptance of the child's saying no sometimes (but doing yes), helps them both endure this difficult phase.

This is the age, too, when, if the ambivalent struggle is very great, the child has very big feelings of anger at mother when she says no. She has to say no almost constantly to her toddler to keep him safe and cared for. Most children will go through some times of difficulty just get-

ting sounds and words out. They go through a phase of
what is documented to be *normal* nonfluency. There are
moments of repetitions and prolongations and struggle
over just making a word, letting it happen. This phenom-
enon has its root here, in the "Shall I, shan't I?" of the
second-year struggle. This nonfluency does not last if it
is met with calm, patient waiting or even with sympathy
for the struggle that is going on. It soon passes as the
child and mother find ways to resolve the difficulty of
feeling two ways at once.

SPEECH DURING THE NURSERY YEARS

By the time the child is 3, if things have progressed
as they ought, the child is able to tell about things, remember what happened yesterday, to organize sentences
long enough to tell what happened—the dog chased him,
or they went to the picnic, or daddy bought a present.
The child has learned that he is a little bit safer in the
world. He can say no to himself if someone is there to
help and he is now ready to branch out a bit. A teacher
can be used as well as mom to be a helper who can show
him things and keep him safe. One of the most helpful
things that can happen at nursery school about speech
and about growing up is the learning how to say the
names of feelings. Some families do this intuitively and
the children arrive at school already doing it, but many
do not. Once this is accomplished the child does not have
to push and shove, he can say, "I want that," or "I didn't
like it that you grabbed me." Words can take the place
of actions. Dr. Anny Katan (1961) described this very
clearly in her publication on the role of verbalization.
The naming of feelings is a great help to a child in being
able to organize his thinking, to know what his feelings
are, and to give him a chance to choose. If he knows, with

words, what he is feeling and thinking, it can give him time to postpone actions and make a choice about what he is going to do. "Shall I grab, shall I say it, or shall I call the teacher?" This also helps him to know what is real and what is not real, and results in better control over his feelings and his impulses.

This is a time when for some children speech is clear and for some it is not. The teacher often wonders whether she should correct what a child is saying or just ignore the problem. This is one of the most frequent questions we get from nursery teachers. The best guide about that is the child himself. How is the child feeling about what he is saying? If his difficulty is interfering with the ability to know what he wants, so that there is a very dramatic interference and he gets frustrated, one should at least acknowledge what has happened. The child needs to know the teacher will figure it out and he should just keep trying until he is understood, because the teacher will be patient. If the child feels very embarrassed, then he needs some help in being shown how to say a word, so he can attempt to repeat it if he wishes. On the other hand, if he just bubbles along and is unaware of the way he has mispronounced the words, and the teacher says to him, "It isn't 'wabbit,' it's 'rabbit'," mostly he is apt to answer, "That's what I said, 'wabbit'." That child is not noticing or caring how he says the word, he just wants to tell about the bunny, and should be answered about the bunny, not about how he says the word. When a mother complains that a child doesn't say the r's right, or doesn't say the s's right, the teacher needs to evaluate the situation in terms of how old the child is and how much it interferes with his communication. How much does he struggle with it? If the child is not really aware of it, is content with the way he gets along with other children and with teachers in the way he talks, it is best not to deal directly with the mispronunciations. The child will only be confused and hurt, perhaps he even might feel he does not want to talk to teachers. Better to explore with the child and the mother how things are between them. Take a look at how the child gets along with his feelings. Does he deal with stressful situations with words or with actions? Work on improving these things can help speech develop at a fairly good rate on its own. If speech remains hard to understand, and begins to cause stress for the child, that is the time to begin to look further.

Different Speech Troubles Need Different Kinds of Help

Should there be speech therapy in nursery school? If it can be the kind that makes talking and communication fun, and does not single out this sound or that word but is designed toward improving communication rather than improving the mechanics of speech, it might be an addition to the classroom. In my opinion these are things that happen anyway in a good classroom with the teacher. If a preschool child's speech is seriously enough disturbed to arouse that much attention, the difficulty lies in the child's personality, not merely in his speech. An evaluation with a specialist in child development, or with a child psychiatrist may be necessary in order to uncover the source of the problem. We need to find out the nature of the difficulty in communication that has brought about the speech trouble. Making such a referral is not an easy thing to do. Many parents would much rather deal with how the child says r's and s's than think about whether or not the way the child talks reflects some other difficulties he may have.

It is rare when a child has a significant trouble with speech, that there isn't some other area where he is also having difficulty, either in getting along with other children or at home with his mother. If the teacher works at it carefully she can get to know the mother well and build a relationship with her where there is trusting communication about what will help the child grow up and feel better; then a referral can be made that would include looking into all aspects of the child's development, not just whether or not the child speaks correctly.

One of the most difficult kinds of speech problem we meet in nursery classrooms is when a child does not want to talk at all. He just will not talk, or will say only minimal things, or will whisper. There can be many reasons for this, but they are not easy to discern by a teacher in the classroom. This problem would be one that would need a referral for evaluation. The difficulty could be related to the child's holding back words because they feel like possessions and parts of himself that he wants to save. It can be that there are some frightening secrets he is afraid he will tell if he talks, there may have been some medical intervention that he fears talking about because it will bring such big feelings he will not be able to stand it. There are as many reasons as there are children who do it, and because it is so major an interference in communication, it is one that needs to be looked into thoroughly.

Another question that needs to be looked at carefully, when a child has a difficulty in speaking, is whether or not there might be a hearing loss. If the child does have a significant hearing loss, then speech, of course, will not develop. Deaf babies do babble in an ordinary fashion but when it comes to that one-year level where the child needs the interaction back and forth with mother, the language development stops. If there is significant deafness, speech will not come on its own. If a child has a moderate hearing loss or a fluctuating loss, then speech may occur, but be difficult to understand. A simple way to judge if there is a hearing loss is to listen for certain key sounds that a child cannot have in his speech if a significant hearing loss exists. If there are no s's, no t's, no f sounds, then a hearing loss should be suspected. If a child does have hearing loss, then speech therapy is helpful and should be provided. I think the child's feelings about having that difficulty should also be shared and understood.

Another question often asked is whether children should be expected to learn two languages at once. Many homes are bilingual. When there are two languages to learn it may take longer for complex use of each language to occur than if there was only one, but children do accomplish this feat better than adults. There are subtle differences between sounds and combinations of sounds used in English and other languages which differentiate two languages for the child. These differences are felt more than they are recognized cognitively.

Teachers are sometimes asked to provide group situations for 2-year-olds whose language is slow to develop, with the hope that being with other children will stimulate speech. This is not a good approach because it is hard for a 2-year-old to be in a group. The thing that helps a 2-year-old with language development most is having good communication with mom. If there are difficulties, finding out what is going on between mom and child is apt to be more helpful than enrolling him in a group. Two-year-olds in groups are mostly going to be wondering where their mother is. But there are some mothers who can care for their children, relate to them, but cannot talk with them. Some of these mothers (and fathers) might be helped by being in a group along with the child. Other mothers who serve as models, along with the help of a supervising person, can sometimes help toddlers begin to talk while in this sharing, caring situation.

Finally, there is the difference between what to do

about speech problems of the school-age child and the preschooler. There is such a difference between these two age groups, yet it is a common idea that whatever you do about speech problems for school-age children, 6, 7, and 8 years old, you should do also with younger children. The school-age child can listen to individual sounds and know they are *part* of a word. They have reached a level of maturity and awareness of themselves so that if they have difficulty with speech, they know they have it and they want to be rid of it. The older child is able to participate in figuring out what is wrong, practicing the sound or sounds, learning a vocabulary of words with those sounds, and monitoring spontaneous speech until the correction becomes habitual. The preschool child, when told he does not say a word right, takes that as a criticism of his whole self and cannot really pick apart a word into sounds. He cannot hear the difference. As described earlier, the child will simply say, "I *said* 'wabbit'," because to him the whole word is the sound. The preschooler cannot sort those things out in speech therapy and so be able to use that kind of help. He can only feel small, dumb, and mad, and rather than helping, such work can be an injury.

To sum up, when a preschooler's speech is hard to understand, this should alert the teacher that something is or has been amiss in communication between mother and child. The teacher can be most helpful when she uses her relationship with the mother to enhance the mother's awareness of the child's point of view and/or to effect a careful evaluation of the nature of this interference by a child development expert.

In the classroom, she helps by listening patiently to the child's struggles to make himself understood. She can offer support and model correct pronunciation, without

requiring the child to repeat, and she assures the child
that speaking will get easier as he grows older.

Chapter 9

The Child with a "Difference" in the Nursery Group

Robert A. Furman, M.D.

In recent years parents and professionals have stressed the advantages of mainstreaming for youngsters with bodily, intellectual, or emotional handicaps, and pre-school settings have increasingly responded in accepting such children. This endeavor has focused interest on how best to help the particular child and his peers to master the concerns they may have about the "difference," so that they will be able to benefit from the educational and social opportunities of the shared nursery group. Many teachers realize that preschoolers are astute observers of even minor differences between themselves and others. Indeed, as educators, we welcome and encourage their ability to observe and compare. But we also recognize that, especially during the nursery years, children are easily bewildered and upset by differences between people, often find it hard to understand what they notice, or even to verbalize their questions and concerns. This applies not only to differences due to illness or anomaly but extends to everything that strikes a young child as unusual, such as unfamiliar ethnic and racial attributes or family constellations which deviate from his norm.

To illustrate the approach we have found most helpful, I shall relate our work with Sally, a 3½-year-old with a mild physical deformity, whose mother made a self-referral to one of the day care centers where I regularly participate as a consultant. The center provides 8 A.M. to 6 P.M. care for the children of working mothers. Children are accepted from age 3 on to about midlatency, say 8 to 10. School-age children go to school from the center and return there after school until the mother comes home from work to pick them up. Experience has taught us to make certain stipulations before accepting a child. Mothers must stay with their child for most of the first three days to ensure a somewhat gradual and guided separation from her. Mothers must come in monthly for conferences with the head teacher or agency director so that impressions of home and school progress can be compared. If difficulties manifest themselves in either area, or rather, when difficulties manifest themselves (as is almost inevitable in this arrangement no matter how well managed), then the mother is expected to come in for weekly consultations until the difficulty has been mastered or understood.

Sally's mother seemed not unusual in seeking admission for her child to the day care center. She had brought her daughter with her, and as she began talking to the director of the center, she suggested to the little girl that she go out and see the school and play with the children, the implication being that the mother could then talk alone with the director. The director stopped this on principle, telling the mother that they could discuss just some practical things that day, and the mother could return alone another day when they would be free to discuss other aspects.

The director, an experienced, skilled nursery school teacher, firmly insisted on this plan for more than reasons of routine. She had noticed that the little girl had deformities of both hands, two fingers in essence missing from each hand. In prior phone contacts the mother had not mentioned the hands, and it appeared as if she was not going to mention them again at this opportunity, although the director was not sure whether the mother wanted the child to leave so she could talk alone with the director about the hands.

When the mother returned alone as planned, the director at once took up the matter with her, saying that the mother had not mentioned about Sally's fingers. The mother acknowledged this, saying that she had become so used to them that she often just forgot about them. The director very sensitively and sympathetically told the mother that the fingers must have brought many hard times and difficult feelings for her. The mother then told of her rather remarkable adjustment to Sally's anomaly, her great initial distress and guilt, her depression in Sally's first few months as she vainly sought explanations for the occurrence of the deformity, and vainly sought someone to blame. When the director commented that she guessed the mother had mostly been blaming herself, the mother relaxed a great deal by observing that the director seemed to know about these things.

She related how she had become so preoccupied with blaming herself that she suddenly discovered that she was even neglecting her child, forgetting the baby in her intense focus on the hands. On her own she most astutely decided this was a great mistake and realized she had to get on with caring for her child, aware that this care might be a bit more difficult than with another child.

The director asked what the mother had told Sally about the hands and the mother described her helpful management. She had told Sally that her hands were different, that they did not know why, and that anyway this was not so important as mother would make sure that she could do all the things that all other children could do. And this was a promise that she had been able to keep, buying clothes, for instance, that did not have buttons or zippers that Sally could not manage, so that the child could dress herself at the appropriate age. And later the mother had spent extra time helping Sally to master buttons.

The director then explained why she had stopped Sally's previous, unannounced visit to the school. She did not want Sally to start with the other children until there had been a chance to prepare the children so that there would be no untoward reactions aimed at Sally from her joining the group. The director then tentatively outlined her plan for this preparation to the mother, a plan she had gone over with me in consultation between the mother's first and second visits. She first explained that her goal was to make sure that this first school experience for Sally went well and that past experience had taught us that if the other children were caught unaware by Sally's deformity they might say nothing about it but evidence their concern or fright by rejecting Sally. She related how very pleased she was that Sally's mother had already discussed the fingers with the child and wondered if the mother would give her permission to say essentially the same thing to the children in the center before Sally came, and to tell the other parents also so that they could be alerted to help their children with questions about Sally, should the questions appear at home rather than at school.

As might be expected of this unusually mature mother, she readily sensed the director had Sally's best interests at heart and agreed to the proposal. One new detail was to be added, and that was to explain to the parents and children that although Sally's hands were different, there was nothing else about her that was different: she would play, argue, laugh, cry, get sad, angry, and excited just like all the other children. The mother agreed to tell Sally that the children would be given this explanation, with the addition I have just noted. The mother was to tell Sally that since her hands would be new and strange to the other children it was good to explain about them so it would not stop the children from becoming the friends and playmates that she wanted so to find in school.

A notice was sent to all the parents, telling of Sally's coming, the explanation that would be given the children before Sally came, the date they would be told, and the date Sally would start. The parents were all urged to consult with the Center if they had questions or if they noted any reactions which they did not know how to manage.

The goal of the reality explanations to parents and children had been twofold: First to give them the facts, and second, and really more important, to establish the idea that Sally's hands were something that no one was going to pretend were different from what they were, and moreover the hands were something that could be talked about by parents or children whenever they might wish.

Little in the way of reactions came directly at first, of course, but there were eventually two notable ones: One little 3-year-old boy in Sally's group had been slowly mastering a bit of a speech impediment and often was rather a silent partner in the group. When Sally joined them he was obviously distressed, staring at her hands, but in his typical fashion saying nothing. Noting his reaction the teacher commented that he looked a bit upset and repeated to him the explanation that had been given beforehand. He looked relieved but said nothing. At lunchtime, sitting across from Sally, he started to mumble, with a severity to his speech impediment that had never been heard in school. His teacher picked this up and said, "Tommy, I think you are still worried about Sally and really don't know how to tell me." To which Tommy replied speaking very clearly, "Tell me again what you said before." His teacher repeated the explanation that Sally's hands were different, that she was born with different hands but that this was the only thing about Sally that was different.

Tommy seemed relieved again, but in a few days, again at lunch, he started spilling and messing at the table as he had never done before, eating in the clumsiest way imaginable. It should be noted that Sally could manage her eating utensils quite adequately. The teacher spontaneously and without particular thought told Tommy that she just could not imagine what was wrong with his hands today. The clumsiness stopped at once, and after lunch, just prior to napping, he was especially close to his teacher. She sensed he had something on his mind and offered him a few minutes on her lap in the corner of the room in case he wanted to tell her something. He readily accepted and sat on her lap wringing his hands. The teacher sensed what it was about and asked him if he were worried about Sally. He said no, but then went on at once, speaking most clearly and anxiously, to say that "Sally's hands were born that way. Her fingers didn't drop off. And mine can't drop off either." His teacher replied, "Of course not Tommy, and now I know what has worried you about Sally. You've been afraid that what happened to her hands could happen to yours." At this point the teacher quite rightly felt that for Tommy the problem of Sally's hands had at last been at least partially mastered. And she turned out to be correct.

The second reaction to Sally was a much briefer one, although nonetheless instructive and interesting. One evening during this period, one of the parents stopped in to chat with the director at closing time, something a bit unusual for this particular mother, so the director was alerted there was something special on her mind. The mother asked about how the class was going and then, apparently apropos of nothing, told about her little girl who had been puzzling them lately at nighttime with rather strange hand-waving movements. The director asked if the girl had spoken at home about Sally, saying that most of the children had in one way or another gotten their parents to repeat at home the same explanation they had been given at school about Sally. The mother was surprised briefly and then said, "Why of course that must be it. I'll go over it with her tonight." She was true to her word and the strange hand movements stopped.

During this period of entry to the Center, Sally's mother met weekly with the director so that she could have some extra help available in case Sally had a hard time with any of the reactions of the children and so that the school staff could keep the mother posted on what transpired at school. The entry went fairly well and Sally, a quite alert little girl with many good play ideas, made a good place for herself among the school group. We felt Sally's gains went beyond just starting her nursery school well. We felt that she was able through the starting school process to solidify the good self-image she had achieved despite her congenital anomaly. We felt the school was able to confirm the excellent approach to her difficulty that her mother had initiated, something that could have been undone or not carried over into the wider school area without the director's and teacher's sensitive approach.

We used this particular approach, and gained the

knowledge which was so readily applied to the work with Sally, her peers, and the parents as a direct result of years of work at the Hanna Perkins Therapeutic Nursery School and Kindergarten (R. Furman and Katan, 1969) where we accept only children with emotional disorders. Through the close liaison between those who teach these preschoolers and those who work with their emotional difficulties, we have had much opportunity to understand how children respond to differences, how this manifests itself in the preschool setting, and how the caring adults can assist them with mastery. I shall select two specific instances from which we learned a great deal: the intensive treatment of a child with a congenital anomaly, and the close observation of many mothers and children when we had to contend in one year in the Hanna Perkins School with the deaths of two mothers, first of a nursery school girl and later of a kindergarten boy (Barnes, 1964; R. Furman, 1964).

To deal with the second of these two instances first, I will refer to some work done by Dr. Marjorie McDonald (1963). When the first mother died, Dr. McDonald began meeting regularly with the teachers to try to pick up through them the children's reactions to their classmate's tragedy. She also met with the therapists who were working with each parent to learn of the reactions that had been visible at home. I want to comment on just two of her many important observations. First, only those children who had some realistic concept of death, of the facts about the end of life, could respond with feeling and in a meaningful fashion; second, when a child responded with feeling he immediately saw the tragedy in reference to himself, when would his mother die? When would he die?

Perhaps the story of a little girl with whose mother I was working at that time will illustrate these points.

When the mother of the nursery school girl died, this little girl, who was in kindergarten, made no comments and asked but one question when she was told by her mother. And this despite the fact she had known the little girl well from out-of-school contacts. She asked her mother where was the mother who had died. Her mother had replied, "In heaven." The mother felt quite mixed about her response because she was not particularly religious, was not sure that she believed what she told her child, and felt that her answer had somehow stopped a meaningful communication. In discussing it with me she decided to go back over this with her daughter and give her a very simple explanation of death as the end of life. She stressed how sad it was, how frightening it was, and what steps the family of the little girl was taking to ensure that all her many needs would be met even though her mother was dead.

Months later when this little girl learned that her classmate's mother had also died, she burst into tears when she was told. She felt so sorry for the little boy. She asked her mother when she, the mother, would die; when she, the little girl, would die. She asked who would take care of the little boy. She asked what she could do to help him. In this discussion she agreed with her mother that maybe all she could do was just tell him in school how sorry she was. This she did, to his great relief as well as that of his classmates who had been feeling the same way but had been too shy to say anything.

With the first death she had acquired the reality facts. With these at her disposal she was able with the second death to respond with feeling, even approaching the obvious, "Could this happen to me also?"

It is not hard to apply these insights to Sally. First, the children had to be given a reality explanation, the facts, so that they would know realistically what they had to deal with and would know there was nothing that could not be talked about. Second, we would not feel that they had mastered the shock of Sally's deformity until they had in some way applied this tragedy to themselves or their family. The little boy who asked his teacher about his fingers was clearly doing this and was thus indicating the degree to which he had assimilated Sally's deformity. He would no longer have to exclude her or be prejudiced against her because he had had the courage and assistance to face the scary question which her presence was sure to evoke—could this happen to me?

How did we know, in explaining Sally's deformity, to emphasize the limits to her difference, the fact that other than for her hands she was just like everyone else, especially in all the feelings that she had? This did not come from intuition, but from the following experience, which took place some time ago. For 3½ years I worked daily in an intensive treatment with a little girl who was born with a sightless and slightly deformed left eye. Her parents had not been able to do what Sally's parents had, that is, discuss the deformity with her. This had been approached only in her treatment with me. Her parents knew she was aware of her deformity at some level because they had seen her before a mirror passing her hands alternately over each of her eyes.

This little girl, whom I called Cindy when I previously described some aspects of her treatment (R. Furman, 1968), had a great deal of trouble with her feelings. She was unable to be sad or angry, with the result that any time she was faced with a situation in which these feelings would normally have appeared, she felt nothing and had an exaggeration of a very bizarre symptom, a severe head rocking. As her treatment progressed we became aware of her trouble with her anger. I remember one day pointing out to her an obvious anger at her mother expressed in a wish that another lady should be stuffed in the trash can and burned up. Cindy was 4 at the time. I told Cindy, that like all little girls, she had just gotten very cross at her mother. She was horrified. She just could not be that angry at her mother. Why if she was angry at her mother she would really wish her dead. I said sure, and it was that way for all little girls sometimes, even though they loved their mothers very much indeed. She said maybe it was true for other little girls but not for her; she was different and her anger was different because her eye was different.

We went through the same process with each feeling, the most dramatic being with her sadness. She did anything and everything to avoid being sad, and it soon became clear it was to avoid crying. Finally one day in her treatment we were discussing her reluctance to accept the fact that her eye "never ever would see," as she used to put it. She burst into tears when I chided her a bit on her reluctance to accept the reality. She ran from the office but returned in a minute smiling through her tears. She had gone to the bathroom to look at herself and had seen that the sightless eye had been crying just like her other eye. "The tear water isn't different; it's just that it doesn't see." She readily agreed that what was important was that, although her eye was different in not being able to see, this was all that was different, that with feelings she was the same as everyone else. Needless to say, this was near the end of her treatment.

In this way Cindy had taught me the importance of what can be called limiting the difference, an observation made by many others, I realize, but one whose poignancy Cindy's experience could never let me forget.

So it was in these ways that the knowledge we found so helpful with little Sally and her classmates about her deformed hands had come to us: first, from the close observations about the children reacting to the tragic deaths of two mothers of preschoolers; second, from the intensive treatment of the little girl with the sightless eye.

It is not easy to help children master differences, even with the help of available knowledge. The director and teachers have to recognize and come to terms with their own reactions. They have to pave the way with parents who are often reluctant to acknowledge the facts or at a loss as to how to address them, and they have to be sensitive to the varied ways in which the children manifest their questions and thoughts. However, it is always a worthwhile educational task which benefits not only the immediate classroom situation but affects many areas of the children's personality development, not least the wish and ability to learn the truth and to accept it without prejudice.

Chapter 10

Children with Toddlerlike Behavior in the Nursery School

Erna Furman

Not infrequently, we find in our nursery school classes youngsters who do not meet the preschool teacher's usual expectations. Most 3–5 year-olds manifest one or another difficulty, but generally function age-appropriately; but there are children, who, though physically fit and well developed, lack the skills for fitting into the small community of the school setting in almost all areas of personality functioning, and we wonder whether they gain anything from attending nursery school. They perplex and annoy us, tax our patience, absorb much of our attention and energy, and are disturbing to their peers. We often label them "naughty," "spoiled," or "difficult," but a closer look shows us that they are actually toddlers. They are of nursery school age but their personalities have not achieved that level. They exhibit the features of a younger child. If they were 2 years old and smaller in stature, we would view them as toddlers, with typical, though perhaps exaggerated, toddler characteristics.

I shall first describe these children's behavior patterns, then discuss some of the causes for the delay or arrest in their development, and last, suggest educational measures we can use to help them and their families. Since we are dealing with a large and complex issue, we cannot hope to exhaust any aspect of it, but we can make a beginning.

WHAT IS TODDLERLIKE BEHAVIOR?

We can often pick out the "toddler" in our nursery group at the very start of the school day. The mother, late, harried, and irritated, may complain how hard it was to get her child ready, how he would not get up, dawdled, did not obey directions and admonitions, insisted on being served a different cereal or on wearing different clothes, played around. She may even confess that, in the end, she or he lost their tempers. While this account clearly describes the youngster's possessive and controlling relationship to his mother before coming to school, once he is at school he usually does not cling but rejects mother instead. He seems oblivious to her presence, and he barely bids her goodbye as he rushes headlong into the toys, frantically explores the materials, pushes into children, or interacts with them impulsively. At the end of the day he is rarely ready to leave, always insists on doing yet another thing, and keeps his mother waiting while she, once again, grows tenser with every minute.

At first, the child may simply ignore us. We hope he will be calmer and more manageable when he gets to know us better but, as he gradually does form a relationship with the teacher, this too becomes a major source of concern. He is as possessive with and demanding of the total person of his teacher as he is with his mother, and forces us to attend to him fully. He achieves this by being contrary, by teasing and provoking, and by engaging us in an endless tug-of-war for power and control. "The moment I take my eyes off him," we say, "he is into something." We quickly realize that verbal contact is ineffective, and we usually do not frustrate ourselves by calling out to him, but find ourselves substituting the bodily contact he seems to need: "Come, take my hand" (as we walk to the outside play area); "Sit next to me" (at story or snack time); and we often put our arm around him for closer intimacy and gentle containment. We also find that we cannot engage his interest in a project with other children or even in working on an activity constructively on his own. Our "toddler" wants to interact with us person to person at all times. As long as we sit and play with him, he can show interest in an activity and enjoy it. But the moment we have to leave or talk to another child, his interest evaporates, the game or material is left in shambles, he himself disappears and soon surfaces in trouble at the other end of the room. This should not surprise us. The child is not yet capable of establishing a teacher–pupil relationship which presupposes pleasure in activities for their own sake and focuses on shared interests and learning of skills. Instead, he relates to us as to a mother-substitute. He enjoys the bodily gratifications of our care, our full devotion to him and his pursuits, and the excited fun of tussling with us over who is boss. For the sake of this infantile, intense relationship he is also willing to join us in the activities *we* like—be it a game, a story, cleaning the tables, or building with blocks—but his enjoyment derives mainly from doing something with us, not from the activity itself or the opportunity to gain knowledge and skill.

Although our "toddler" can be very loving and affectionate, we soon come to appreciate that his relationship with the mother-substitute, as with his mother, is devoid of concern for his loved ones and does not mitigate his primitive ways of showing anger. The loved teacher may be attacked physically and/or abused verbally in response to the least frustration. Or, in an attempt to preserve the teacher's good graces, the child's anger may be split off from her and redirected to targets he cherishes much less—peers, assistants, newcomers, even toys and furniture. In some instances, the "toddler's" anger is divided between home and school. He may give mother a loving goodbye but strike out at others as soon as she leaves, or he may be fairly cooperative with the teacher but mean to mother on the way to and from school.

The child's primitive and often misdirected anger is, of course, not the only area in which he lacks means of inner control. The basic educational tenets of "not this but that," "not here but there," and "not now but later" impinge upon him as demands from his environment, but they have not yet become a part of his own personality and do not serve him as internal guides toward self-discipline. Every no is an infuriating interference because he lacks frustration tolerance. He cannot wait his turn at the slide because he cannot bear any delay in gratifying a need or wish. If he wants a particular truck to play with, no other will do, because he cannot accept substitutions. His pleasures are immediate, bodily, and instinctual, and as yet not channeled into neutral activities which often require patience and effort. Thus we find him messing with paint instead of using it to create a picture, bashing down or throwing around blocks instead of making a structure, barging into people and things with his tricycle instead of mastering the skill of guiding it around them. His concentration span is usually quite limited, so that even favorite activities, like water and sand play, tend to deteriorate unless closely supervised. He may command a considerable vocabulary and speak fluently, but does not use language for effective communication of ideas or for recognition and mastery of feelings. Instead, he discharges inner tensions bodily, in frequent bouts of uncontrolled motility, in many trips to the bathroom, or in wiggling restlessly, and conveys a general impression of "ants in the pants."

WHAT ARE THE CAUSES OF THIS DEVELOPMENTAL LAG OR ARREST?

During the toddler phase, between the ages of 1½ to 2½ or 3 years, many inner and outer factors interact to pave the way for mastering the age-appropriate developmental steps. But there is one factor which contributes most significantly to the child's growth toward considerate relationships, increased inner controls, and the capacity to form a teacher–pupil relationship: It is a continuous and good enough relationship with a mothering person who herself functions at a mature level. Such a relationship may be interfered with in a number of ways and may then fail to meet the toddler's crucial developmental need.

Interference may be caused by breaks in the relationship: permanent breaks, due to the death of the mother, due to adoption, divorce, or changes in foster care; or temporary breaks of sufficient impact, due to illness, working hours, or parental vacations. A break in the relationship may also happen when the mothering person is physically present but mentally absent, as in the case of maternal depression or emotional withdrawal, perhaps related to overriding concerns in the mother's current life circumstances.

Double or multiple parenting, unless carefully and sensitively gauged with a view to minimizing its stresses, may similarly interfere with the child's need for a consistent one-to-one relationship. This can happen when family members share too prominently in the daily care of the child (fathers, grandmothers, aunts), when nannies, baby-sitters, or neighbors are regularly employed, or when the youngster spends time in a group setting, such as a day care center.

Sometimes the interference lies, not in discontinuity, but in the nature of the mother's relationship with her toddler. Most of us get occasionally seduced into acting like a toddler with a toddler. He can, at times, engage us in his tug-of-wars or provoke us to undue anger and childish retaliation. With some mothers, however, these are not occasional lapses but pervasive personality difficulties. When a mother herself lacks inner controls, when anger is always a prominent part of her relationships, and when she is compelled to struggle for power and control with her child, she may exaggerate rather than mitigate his toddler ways and interfere with his maturation.

Traumatic events, too, may play an important role; for example, the toddler may be ill and may have to undergo painful treatments. This may increase his anger, exaggerate his feelings of helplessness, and immobilize his means of coping to such an extent that even a helpful mother may be unable to alleviate his stress sufficiently.

HOW CAN WE HELP THESE CHILDREN IN THE NURSERY SCHOOL?

We may be tempted to think that a lag in development will correct itself in time. On that basis, we may wish to delay the child's entry to nursery school by half a year or more, or we may decide to keep him, in the hope that he will improve spontaneously as he gets older. Unfortunately, time alone does not overcome such developmental hang-ups, even when the specific events or situations which caused them are no longer operative.

The child's difficulties may actually worsen as he gets older, in part because the toddlerlike behavior becomes increasingly inappropriate at later stages, in part because the child cannot master the subsequent developmental steps with the limited tools of his 2-year-old personality, so that new troubles constantly pile up on top of old ones.

It is not easy for the teacher to devote the necessary time and energy to helping the "toddler" in her nursery group, but it is the only constructive way of approaching his troubles.

BUILDING A RELATIONSHIP WITH OUR "TODDLER"

Our task begins at the very start, by helping the child to separate from his mother and to get to know the nursery as a safe place with a trustworthy mother-substitute. Experience shows us that we cannot achieve these goals by simply asking the mother to remain at the school a little longer or by telling the child that he is missing mommy and is sad without her. Without special help, the "toddler" cannot use mother's presence in a constructive way, nor does he long for her when she is absent. His problem is more primitive. It lies, first and foremost, in his difficulty in keeping his mother in his mind and heart and in feeling that she can still care about him when she is not actually interacting with him. We try to correct this "out of sight, out of mind" attitude by bringing the mother into the nursery school indirectly, through words, concrete reminders of her, and contacts with her during the school day. Thus, we ask the mother for her daily schedule and, throughout the day, we frequently and spontaneously talk to the child about his mom's activities and feelings about him. "I bet your mom is thinking about you now. She is at her office (factory, etc.), doing such and such, but she also thinks to herself, 'My Johnny is with Mrs. Smith at school. I love him. I wish I could be with him. I can't wait to see him again.' And when she comes to pick you up, we'll tell her that you built with blocks (had crackers for snack, put on your own boots, etc.)." We also ask the mother to leave one of her personal belongings with her child—her scarf, gloves, belt, sweater, hat, old purse, or some item from its contents. The child can carry these "pieces" of mom with him wherever he goes or keep them in his cubby. We encourage him to use them as valuable reminders: "What did your mom leave with you today? Want to show me? Oh, what a beautiful hat! That's nice to have with you. It tells you she really likes you." Photographs of the mother or the child's own soft toys do not serve the same purpose but may be of additional help. Similarly, we may suggest that the child choose something of his to give to mom so that she can keep it in her pocket or purse to think of him: a little scribbled drawing, a toy, a little doll, a special stone or acorn he found. When we explain to the mother how important she is to her child, even though he does not act like he cares, and how much he needs to keep in touch with her mentally, we can enlist her help. She can tell him where she is during his school hours and describe what she does. She can help him have a clearer idea in mind by showing him her place of work (or where she takes classes, shops, visits, etc.). She can assure him that she does indeed think of him and care about him even when she is not with him. Many mothers are able to follow our suggestion to keep in touch by phoning the child at school and/or by making a telephone number and time available so that the teacher can help the child to call her. Some teachers have successfully encouraged mothers to visit with the child at school, to join him at the school luncheon, to take him home earlier on their day off. This is especially helpful when the nursery is a day care center and mother's absence encompasses long hours. Mother can also assist by making sure that she is always the one to bring and pick up her child, because even the most beloved substitute (father, grandmother) is still a substitute. When the child has to pass from one substitute to another substitute his stress is greatly increased. The mother who herself brings and fetches her child may at times reap a reward of extra rambunctiousness or obstinacy, but that just shows how much she means to him. We do not get angry at people that do not matter to us.

The teacher's efforts at helping her "toddler" to keep his mother in mind are one of the ways she builds a relationship with him. There are other ways, too. Above all, and as much as possible, she keeps her "toddler" close by physically—sitting next to her, holding her hand, playing within her arm's reach, or with her arm around his chair—and she makes sure she takes him along wherever she goes. At the same time she reminds him in words that she is in touch, with a comment on his clothes or on his activity, with a reminder when things seem to "fall apart," with a bit of praise when he does well, with a remark about his mom, a question about home, or by preparing him for the next step in the school routine. And when she talks with or helps other children, she most especially lets him know that she continues to be aware of him and of his need of her. Only after weeks, or even months, is it possible to extend the bodily distance between teacher and child and to substitute a mental link of words and eye contact. "I see you at the other table." "You can come over and show me what you did." "Do you like the puzzles I put out on the shelf there?" Needless to say, these children are not helped by being passed on to another teacher and require special preparation and help when such changes are unavoidable during the school day.

In addition to close contact, the child's special teacher makes sure, from the start, that he knows what her main job is, namely to keep the nursery a safe place. She does so in word and deed; she protects him and his belongings from others, and she quickly restrains him from hurting people and things. "I won't let you hurt anyone or anything and I won't let anyone hurt you and your things. We have a rule that our nursery school has to be safe and it's my job to help everybody keep this rule." She also explains that the grown-ups have to stick to this rule, that they do not spank or hit, but stop children in other ways—by holding them, by not letting them play in some areas, or with some peers or equipment. It is often necessary to distinguish home and school rules in this respect because the parents of these children may use physical punishment as their only available "weapon." When the teacher has been unable to prevent the youngster from abusing a toy or person, she has to spend time and effort in helping him to make up, to put things right—a little service or picture for the injured peer, Scotch taping the torn book, picking up the strewn-around blocks.

When our "toddler" begins to tease us, we know that his relationship to us is beginning to grow. We recognize that for him, as for all toddlers, teasing is *the* way of loving. We are, of course, tempted to respond at his level; that is, to get provoked and to join him in his excited tug-of-war. It helps to acknowledge in words, but not in deed, his wish to feel close through teasing. This is when we have to make a special effort to maintain our more mature ways of relating and offer him the opportunity to join *us* at our level instead. When the provocative gleam in his eye tells us that he runs off in order to be chased, or balks at clean-up to create a struggle, we may say, "I like you, too, but this is no fun for me. When I like people I like to play a game together or talk with them. Only very little kids tease and fight and chase. Soon you'll get to be bigger and then you'll want to have more grown-up fun with me." Of course, we use every chance to welcome and praise moments when the child can show his fondness in a more mature way; for example, when he helps us with a chore or cooperates in routines and activities. "It's so nice when you can be so big and we can have a nice time together. It's a lot more fun than teasing."

USING OUR RELATIONSHIP TO HELP OUR "TODDLER" GROW

As our relationship with the child becomes stronger, we begin to use it to further his personality growth in important areas. It is most important that we use the relationship to help the child direct and modify his anger appropriately. Toddlers need to learn that we do get angry at the very people we love most and that, because we love them, we make sure our anger does not hurt them. Some youngsters attack us physically the moment we disappoint or frustrate them. We learn to be on the lookout for such behavior and to hold them at bay to prevent injury. "I won't let you hurt me. I know you're angry but you like me, too. We don't hurt those we care about. I tell *you* when I'm angry and you can tell *me*." His enraged reply may be an attempt at an extra hard kick and/or an outburst of, "You are mean. I hate you," but that need not floor us. "Right now you think you're only mad at me, but you do have good feelings, too, and you'll find them again."

Often the child's anger at us is vented on others—peers

or other teachers. Time and again, Denise would suddenly push another child or knock down his building. Closer observation revealed that these outbursts followed her teacher's turning to another child, thwarting Denise's wishes, or interfering with her activities. Once the teacher recognized these connections, she would quickly help Denise to redirect her anger to its true target. "Why, Denise, it's *my* fault that I said 'no' to you," or, "I am the one who went to talk to Jimmy." "*I* let Mary play with the dolls today." "You are angry at *me*, not at him. Come and tell *me*." As with many such children, Mondays or other times after the teacher's "time off" were especially hard. Denise seemed to feel that her teacher had rejected and deserted her when absent, and she "paid her back" by attacking others.

In a similar way, the "toddler's" anger at his mother is often displaced to the teacher or school and when he feels angry at the teacher he may, likewise, "take it out" on mother. The start and end of the day is, for this reason, often especially troublesome. No sooner has mother left in the morning but the child attacks the teacher or interferes with peers, and if the teacher made him angry in the last part of the school day, mother may be faced with a difficult son or daughter at pick-up time. The teacher can help by pointing out in the morning, "You get so mean with us when mom leaves. Perhaps you are mad at her for leaving you. You can tell me when you are angry at mom and I'll help you tell her too. She won't mind. She still likes you. She'll understand that it's hard not to be with her." At the end of the day, she may indeed need to help her pupil verbalize his feelings to mother, but she may also need to redirect his anger from mother back to herself if it seems that she is the one who crossed him. Anger can only become modified and channeled into words when it is felt and expressed to the right person about the right thing.

Building inner controls and masteries is another important area we address via our relationship with the child, who learns to bear frustrations, to wait, to compromise, to forego pleasures; to share, to be kind and considerate; to enjoy activities that do not provide immediate bodily fun but require patience, skill, and perseverance; to take pride in his achievements and to play or practice on his own; as well as learning to modify his anger and express it in words. From the child's viewpoint, all these goals and accomplishments are only worth striving for when his loved adult enjoys them herself, and with him; when she supports and admires every little step he takes; when she expects these goals and accomplishments from him and conveys trust that he can achieve them. The teacher, therefore, not only tells the youngster that "waiting" is one of the things that bigger people can do and that he still needs to practice it, but she adds that she is sure he will soon be able to manage waiting better and will then feel so proud of himself. And when an occasion arises where he has been able to wait a few seconds, she points it out: "Hey, I just saw you wait for me (or, wait for your turn). You are getting to be a good 'waiter.' That's great! You must feel good to be able to do such a big-boy thing. We'll tell mom. She'll be glad to hear about it, too." Although we share, and let mom share, in the pleasure of each little step, we stress how good it must feel to the child so that his achievements can become a source of self-esteem and self-confidence for him, a base for further positive growth. With children who so often inevitably hear comments about their shortcomings and failures, it is especially important to spot even the tiniest improvement, a basis for his hope for himself. Lack of trouble can easily go unnoticed, particularly by the child, and requires the teacher's watchful eye and emphasis.

CAN WE HELP THE PARENTS?

The "toddler's" parents are often too harassed, embarrassed, exasperated, and defensive to want to listen to advice. Like their "toddlers," they may hate to be "told what to do" even when they feel helpless. A little empathy for how hard it is to get Johnny to and from school and for how much parents always try and wish all would go well with their child, may be enough for a good start. Enrolling mother in our initial program of keeping the child in touch with her during the school day may help to some extent in letting her know that we feel her child cares about her a lot, even though he does not seem to show it. Beyond that, I find it best to let the parents make their own observations of the teacher's methods. If and when they bring about some improvement, the mother will notice them, too, and may even try to follow our lead. When she asks how we deal with certain situations or why we approach them as we do, we explain, adding that it takes a long time but has helped other children with similar troubles. We are hopeful for her child, too. In time, some mothers share more of their concerns and ask for conferences to learn more about the school's methods and about ways in which they could be applied at home. Some parents with special interest, and perhaps special home problems, may even get to the point of accepting a referral in order to work with a specialist in childhood problems. Referral is especially indicated when the parents want to be active in helping their child and when we know, or have reason to surmise, that specific past stressful events interfered with the child's development. Some parents, however, may remain more remote and skeptical, hesitate to take steps toward supporting our work, and have great difficulty in adopting some of our approaches. In any case, it always takes much tact and time on our part and a continued willingness to give the parents a chance.

HOW MUCH CAN WE HELP SUCH "TODDLERS?"

At best, improvements are slow and results may be limited. Our efforts, however, are most worthwhile. Every little progressive step not only spells relief for the teacher but represents an important gain for the child and facilitates his means of "self-healing"; that is, his potential for maturation.

The outlook is most hopeful when we can, in time, enlist the parents' help so that school and home can work together along the same lines. When we can assist a child only at school, his chances for success are inevitably less good. However, the mere opportunity to experience another way of coping with the world, with the help of a devoted teacher, can make a difference. It may help to provide the child with a safe, less troubled, place. It may take him a bit further toward mastering feelings and help him gain some pleasure in achievement. The child's relationship with us may establish the idea of school as a good place and may pave the way toward his better acceptance of teachers and school settings in the future, based on his experience with us. Whenever we can contribute positively to a child's growth during his preschool years we are more effective than when similar help is offered only at a later stage in his development.

The following four case examples will illustrate how the troubles of such children were understood and worked with—some more, some less successfully. The two children described by Arthur L. Rosenbaum exemplify the ways in which we work with, understand, and help children at the Hanna Perkins Therapeutic Nursery School. The two children described by Maria Kaiser show how we apply what we have learned to assist children in other preschool settings where we participate as regular consultants to the director and educational staff.

Chapter 11

Toddlerlike Behavior: Two Case Examples—1

Arthur L. Rosenbaum, M.D.

In describing the work with two children and their parents, I shall focus on the troubles they encountered on entering the Hanna Perkins Therapeutic Nursery School, what was observed, and what could be understood, and how that understanding led to measures that were helpful.

The children, Peter and Helen, share some attributes. They are similar in that each brought to the new nursery school situation many qualities of the toddler phase which, each for his or her own reason, had not been fully completed. Each of them had parents who were fully functioning, and families where basic physical and psychological needs had been adequately met. There had been no early separations and all substitute caretakers had been well known to the mothers. Whatever disturbances that had to be addressed were within the relationship between child and mother. Although one of the children had had an accident, the memory of which did affect his reaction to the new experience of school, both children reflected, more than anything else, the nature of this most important relationship in their behavior. It is for these reasons that these children were selected as examples of the kind of toddler difficulties often seen in nursery schools.

A brief account of how entry into Hanna Perkins School is accomplished will help you to appreciate the context in which these events unfolded. Although each child and mother may require some variation in timing to meet their particular needs, the general procedure at Hanna Perkins is to set aside the first few weeks of school as a time when the physical and mental tasks of leaving the mother behind to come to school are most important. We recognize that even the child who is mentally ready to enter and benefit from nursery school, has but recently acquired a degree of independence in body care and in the capacity to enjoy the experiences of relating to others. These achievements are still potentially vulnerable to being overwhelmed. The child's capacity to become acquainted and relate to entirely new people remains largely dependent upon the nature of his relationship to the mother and family. This relationship has been most recently the relationship of a toddler. The mother is the most important person in helping her child with the new task: through her physical and emotional availability, through her understanding of her child's thoughts and feelings, and her ability to assist him in mastery. Consequently, enough time is set aside for the mother to be in the classroom with the child; later, for her to be in the school and easily available to the child; still later for her to be away part of the time, but part of the time present, so that each small step and new experience can be introduced and carefully considered by the mother. She is helped by the teachers and in her weekly interviews with the therapist, but it is primarily through her that the child learns to relate to the new teacher as a teacher, instead of viewing her as a mother-substitute, and can thus truly accomplish entry into the school.

Peter was 4½ when he began school at Hanna Perkins. Four-and-a-half-year-olds are not usually expected to be as plagued by these troubles as was Peter. This was not his initial school experience. He had attended another nursery school for nearly a year, but even that was his second experience. The first one lasted only three days. On the way to that school the first day he and his mother encountered an accident. They were not involved, they only passed by, but police cars with sirens and lights were much in evidence. Peter introduced himself to the school by crashing into other children and dashing immediately to the top of the jungle gym. His mother, familiar with such reactions and anxious about them, tried to interest the teacher in the events. She felt she wasn't heard. The teachers encouraged her to leave but Peter clung to her. When the same behavior occurred for the next two days, they left the school. At the second school the teachers were more helpful but, although Peter's behavior was calmer, everyone was concerned about him. Within three months an evaluation, suggested by the teacher, was completed and the mother began to work with a therapist.

In that school Peter attacked and frightened smaller children and ones who would not defend themselves. He grabbed things from others and often felt bad and cried about his inability to stop himself from these attacks. His speech was often hard to understand as it could become rapid and garbled. He was afraid of the janitor's vacuum cleaner and anxiously watched and listened for it, crying and attacking when he heard or saw it. At home, he attacked his younger brother. The parents said that they had earlier consulted a pediatrician about these attacks and understood him to say to spank Peter each time he hit his brother. The family conscientiously followed this unhappy advice and Peter had daily spankings. During that school year as the work progressed, the spankings stopped and a referral to the Hanna Perkins School was made. By the time Peter entered, his mother was pregnant. The attacks on other children had ceased; he now could speak of his wish to hurt his brother, and each week awaited the arrival of the garbage truck on his street, exhorting his parents to place his brother in it. The vacuum cleaner was no longer a source of terror.

When he met his new teachers at the Hanna Perkins School he impressed them with his capable behavior. They soon learned that if he had warning of new situations he could handle them. However, he tested the rules constantly, and initially he was interested in but two activities—he crashed cars excitedly or calmly played with a tractor he rode about on. He began each day with this play, only gradually involving himself with other children. Initially his play with others was with dolls. He played at taking them to the hospital. Later he played with others at being a repairman of some kind. As his mother left the nursery, transitions which had been manageable while his mother was there became times of anxiety. With each one he told a scary story and made siren noises. When his mother left the school for brief walks he busied himself so as not to notice her absence, and upon her return he refused to acknowledge her. When he was not supervised by a teacher or his mother he would ride too fast, climb too high, and was unsafe with equipment. At story time, he seemed lonely, tending to lean close to others, wanting to sit with his arm around another. The teachers were surprised to observe that he knew verbatim many of the books they read. He anticipated out loud each event in the story. His teasing as he grew more uncomfortable in the school became incessant, and in one way or another he was able to disrupt any activity he was a part of. These disruptions were often subtle and disowned by him.

I think that I have described enough to indicate the basis for my next remark. Peter, at 4½, upon entry to the school, attempted to make things tolerable for himself by controlling his environment. This behavior is in sharp contrast to what is ordinarily expected of a child of 4½ whose development permits age-appropriate behavior. Such a child might vie for the teacher's attention, to be well thought of, to be first in line, the best behaved, showing off skills and accomplishments. Peter's manner of dealing with things was more typical of a younger child whose approach to life is marked by the necessary and age-appropriate task of mastery of his body and its functions. This indicated that Peter had encountered interferences during his earlier development that did not now permit more appropriate relationships to help him make things more manageable. In fact, it was some time before we learned that he had not yet achieved mastery over his body functions in that his mother continued to assist in cleaning him after he used the toilet. It is not hard to realize how a child could be so uncomfortable away from his mother if he could not take care of his body, let alone his impulses.

Peter, as indicated above, had not only seen an accident but experienced one himself. At 20 months, a month after his brother was born, Peter had suffered a fracture. Although the specific details of the injury and its treatment relate directly to many aspects of his symptomatic behavior, it is enough to say here that his ability to control his own body, let alone events, had been overwhelmed. The entry into a new school, as well as his mother's pregnancy, provided the circumstances that made it necessary for him to further understand and master many of his memories and the frightening feelings connected with them. However, there were other, even more influential determinants of his behavior that became clearer as the work with the parents continued. Our knowledge of these determinants was gained over many months of hard work. It became clear in time that both of Peter's parents responded to upsets within themselves by making others, including and especially Peter, upset. Peter was doing in school what had been done to him at home, and his parents were unknowingly doing to him what had been done to them. This made their conscientious use of the spankings more understandable. They attempted to make themselves calmer by attempting to control him with the spankings. It may be that this mechanism was what prompted the first nursery school teacher to encourage the mother to leave on Peter's first school day.

The work with Peter's parents around the management of their own anxiety was crucial. Peter's adjustment to school was made possible by the teacher's ability to interact with him in a way that did not perpetuate his need to control. Peter had to be reminded often of the inner origin of his scary feeling, that at school such behavior was not permitted, that infringement of rules would not lead to struggles or attacks on him but to consistent discipline. He was, for example, asked to remove himself from group activities if his teasing disrupted them, to compensate those he injured with his cruel verbal attacks with drawings and notes of apology, to use his urges for activity toward completing a task, doing a puzzle, or a job. Through this work that went on for many months, he was able to become a schoolchild much more interested in the world around him.

Although he was helped considerably and his development progressed, it eventually became clear, when he was older and adjusting to even more demanding school situations, that a direct treatment of his troubles was necessary.

Helen was 3½ when she entered the Hanna Perkins School. She had been regarded since her birth as the thorn in her brother's existence. As she grew older she could not be kept out of his room or out of his things. She could not be kept in her room for naps unless her door was locked. Early attempts at toilet training were no more successful, and admitting defeat in the face of Helen's growing obstinacy and teasing, the mother had put her back in diapers when she was 2½. The mother's feeling of desperation in the face of this prompted her to want to begin to work on the trouble.

Helen's parents were very much invested in their children. There were no interests in their lives that were more important to them. However, it appeared that neither parent could make clear and consistent demands that indicated to the children that they were expected to master their own urges. They often expressed their love to the children in ways that interfered with mastery. They were indulgent in doing for the children rather than expecting them to do for themselves. They were often unwittingly overstimulating as they permitted, or invited, the children into the bedroom or bathroom or continued body care functions for the child beyond the time when such functions could have been taken over by the child. A further complication was that they had earlier sought and obtained advice and had complied superficially with the recommendations that modesty and privacy in bedroom and bathroom should be observed. Although they complied, they resented what they regarded as the imposition of another's standards upon them; at the same time they knew that the children were calmer because of the changes they had made. The im-

provement heightened their awareness of their responsibility and their guilt. They repudiated their previous
behavior and acted as if it had never existed. Looked at
in this way, Helen's troubles seemed understandable. She
was permitted, even encouraged, to express what her parents wished to express, but out of guilt hid from their
awareness.

The crisis came over Helen's refusal to use the potty.
The mother was not able to make clear and consistent
her demand that Helen remain clean. Helen seemed to
enjoy the struggle that went on between them. When we
closely examined the struggle we found that the task of
using the potty remained largely that of the mother. She
repeatedly reminded Helen that she should use the potty,
but Helen never had to use it until too late. The mother
continued to clean up the mess because Helen could never
get it right. It seemed paradoxical that Helen, who could
not clean herself, flush the toilet, dispose of the soiled
clothing in the proper place, or wash her hands, could
manage to open or unlock any door or drawer in the house.

One day, when Helen was 3, as they waited to pick
up her big brother at school, Helen told her mother, "Big
girls don't poop in their pants." From that day on she did
not soil again, although struggles around eating, dressing, and at bedtime continued.

Helen began school at that point. She alternated between sitting in her mother's lap and playing while
mother was in the room. When it was time to leave, the
mother had trouble doing so promptly and dragged out
goodbyes. In her mother's absence, Helen spoke often of
missing her. She was unable to concentrate on any activity for very long. She soon appeared tired, sucked her
thumb, and lowered her head to the table. Her play very
quickly became silly, soon consisting of rolling and gig-
gling on the floor. When supervised by her teacher she

could enjoy activities. Although she attempted to engage the teacher in struggles, she could regain control when reminded of the expectation for school behavior. When her mother returned to pick her up Helen again struggled and between them, it took as much as 30 minutes to leave the school.

In the work with the mother the therapist could contribute nothing that seemed useful. It became clear that the therapist had to deal with an obstinacy in the mother that was little different from that of the child.

Helen's difficulty in making the transition to school was part of a problem in her relationship with her mother. The problem between them was not easily, if at all, soluble. Yet Helen was capable of becoming a schoolgirl. The teacher's efforts at making age-appropriate demands in a consistent manner, avoiding interactions that became struggles, making expectations clear and firm, allowed Helen to realize other aspects of her personality. The teacher's helpful example and the work with the mother did allow the mother the opportunity to identify within herself some aspects of the interaction that could be changed. Without the school experience it is doubtful that Helen and her mother could have known that there were other ways of interacting.

Helen and Peter had not been able to master those tasks ordinarily expected of preschoolers at the time of entry to nursery school. Each sought comfort in the school in a toddlerlike relationship similar to that which existed at home with their mothers. Observing the process of separation enabled the teachers to get to know the children and mothers and to learn more about the difficulties. Ways were found to help the children experience new approaches, mastery, and in time, a more age-appropriate teacher–pupil relationship. To resolve the children's disturbances and improve the parent–child relationships required long and painstaking therapeutic work, but in the meantime, school had become more pleasurable for its own sake, rather than because it represented a struggle for control.

Chapter 12

Toddlerlike Behavior: Two Case Examples—2

Maria Kaiser

The children I am about to describe were both observed in a health care center playroom. This room looked
very much like a nursery school class and was used by
parents coming to the clinic. It was in this room they
could leave their children as they or one of their family
members was being seen by a doctor. Within this setting
we set up a program for parents and children that met
twice a week for approximately two hours in the morning.

Joshua was one of the first referrals. He arrived with
his mother when he was 2 years, 3 months old, referred
by a pediatrician who had listened to the mother express
apprehension about her ability to care for this 2-year-old.
There was some concern, too, because he was still drink-
ing from a bottle.

"Joshua always has to have his own way," the mother
said. "He doesn't listen to anything I say, refuses to have
anything to do with being toilet trained, jumps up and
down, and yells a lot when I tell him 'no,' makes a mess
of the house, eats whenever and whatever he chooses."
She said her nerves were bad and the advice she was

getting from her mental health caseworker was dealing with her problems and not with Joshua's problems!

This was a mother with a history of foster care placements and agency dependency. Her natural family, living nearby, had been plagued with mental health problems, hearing impairments, and two of her siblings had been diagnosed as retarded. This was a mother who had spent many weekend and evening hours in hospital emergency rooms, terrified Joshua might have swallowed something toxic, have a cold which would never get better, or a sore that would never heal. She was most anxious always to be near someone who would help her with the overwhelming task of dealing with a child.

They were always on time or early. She arrived with a face full of sadness and a body to match. She was pregnant with her second child. Joshua was a well-coordinated child of average size with a wide-eyed, bewildered look. When mother put him down out in the hall, for she frequently carried him everywhere, he would burst through the playroom door, fling his little doll off into some corner, never to be retrieved, peel off his outer garments, which stayed where they fell, and proceed to flit from blocks to beads, puzzles to doll dishes, trucks to crayons. In the beginning he made a pool of pieces of toys through which he would kick or swim. His mother would either leap ahead of him, thwarting his every move, or more often she would sit dejectedly staring out the window, a million miles away. Occasionally she would "come to" and call out, "No, no, no," or "Joshua, Joshua, Joshua," without ever checking to see where he was or what he was doing.

When he wanted something he would complain and whimper and pull on her clothing. The only words I heard were, "BEBE, pickee up, Noopie," and "Who is it?" The rest of the time he garbled his words. It was a series of sounds which flowed with expression and were accompanied by what seemed like appropriate facial and body gestures. I would ask for a translation and would be told he was talking about something he had seen on television, a trip downtown, or a visit to her mother's house. He would "talk," point, and gesture, and then go off in a direction other than the one indicated, without a backward glance to see if he had my attention or if I were following. He made no use of the adults in the room. There was no conversation between this child and his mother. He did not react to "Look," or "Let's get the ball to play with," or "Here are some cars."

I thought something was wrong with his hearing, and the referral was made; needless to say his ears were working very well.

From the beginning I had insisted that the mother play with us—help with the puzzles, have a cup of coffee in the doll corner, help set up the bowling pins, and so on. Joshua really helped me with this, for he always returned to the very toys he had played in the company of his mother the last time, and pointing this out to her each time would encourage her to keep it up. We also discovered she really liked materials with which she could make patterns, thus, we made sure these were provided, for she would then stay with us and Joshua would play with the same things alongside her.

Puzzled by the lack of use of language, I brought a description of this child for consultation to our "Nursery School Children with Difficulties" seminar which is held every other week at the Cleveland Center for Research in Child Development.

To learn to make use of words a child needs to have someone with whom he has a relationship to respond to his efforts at communication. In this case, the mother had been so preoccupied with her own troubles, she simply did not hear this child. He did have access to a television which was on all day and so was quite familiar with thousands of sounds which really were given no meaning. Regardless of the feelings of the child as he watched, the television went on and on, unresponsive to his moods of anger, sadness, or joy.

The recommendation was a nursery school or day care program where he could experience a number of different activities, including eating, and where the mother would also be welcome and attend with the child. It was hoped that a strong, sensitive, capable teacher could provide a caring and teaching model for both and, within this relationship, Joshua's language and use of materials would be encouraged. A nursery school was found with a teacher possessing all these superb qualifications.

All the problems did not, of course, disappear, but Joshua's language and communication skills soared. Within a year he could say whatever he wanted to, could talk to other children and adults, and could express many of the well-known feelings: "I'm mad. I don't like it. That's nice."; and he functioned much more age-appropriately.

Lannie was one of seven children born to a large, handsome, very verbal woman who also had experienced many foster care placements as she was growing up. The mother had no knowledge of her natural family and claimed to have been abused in many of the homes where she stayed. She frequently brought all seven of her children into the playroom in the health care center—sometimes to leave them as she kept appointments with her doctor or with one of her children's pediatricians. Many times she came simply to visit. She not only found great satisfaction visiting with her adult friends in the playroom, but also watched as her children made productive use of the playroom materials. Ranging in age from 3–12, they would spread out, filling the room. One needed to be at one's best, for some of their entertainment consisted of helping themselves to materials being used by others or examining areas in the room which had been designated as "off limits," but generally speaking, most of the time they were gainfully employed. Their mother, very aware of this activity, watched with pride, bragged about their particular abilities, and was careful to gather any paintings or drawings to take home with her. She frequently described other programs at church or in the community which she and the children would attend.

Lannie was the one child who did not make use of this room. At age 4, she came in the room with the group, glued to her mother, and refused to become unstuck. The corners of her mouth pulled down, her eyes knit together so closely you could barely see them, and her message, when and if she looked your way was, "Don't come near me." Her mother would chide her and suggest activities, but when it did not work, did not insist but kept her close. As long as this was a visit, one felt badly she was not able to enjoy the room as her brothers and sisters did. But the mother was not encouraging intervention either. It was when mother had to leave the room that the explosion came. Lannie screamed and cried, she thrashed out at everyone who came near her, including staff members she had seen on a regular basis since birth, as well as her siblings who occasionally tried to help. She did not let up until the mother returned. Frequently, mother expecting this, had waited, listened, and returned to the room to retrieve her. Other times Lannie spent furious and raging until her mother returned.

Why was this child so very angry, so unapproachable, so unable to make use of any of the materials in this room or to talk with or enjoy the adults and other children?

Here again I brought the problem to the discussion group. Discussed was the fact that twice in this child's first year the mother had been hospitalized and therefore separated from her. They had moved from one city to another and from one house to another within the city. There were a number of children in the home in whom the mother had had to invest, and perhaps for some reason she had invested excessively in the younger brother, with little time or energy for Lannie. Perhaps the mother's need to have one child so dependent on her was perpetuating this behavior. However Mrs. Furman, our consultant, kept returning to a curiosity about what had taken place in the toddler phase, or between ages 2 and 3. It seemed as if, even though there had been incidents which might serve to weaken this child's defenses, that there *had* to have been a traumatic incident during the toddler stage.

I returned to the records and again went through them. There it was: When Lannie was 2½ she had been placed, feet first, in a tub of scalding hot water, and the second-degree burns on the bottom of her feet had to be treated in a hospital emergency room with follow-up care for the next two weeks at the health care center.

Since this family was not seen on a regular basis, it was some weeks before I saw four of them at the clinic, Lannie, and her 3- and 6-year-old brothers. During the greeting and ensuing conversation, I said to Lannie, "I understand you really had a frightening thing happen to your feet when you were just 2." "Yes!" came a quick response from the 6-year-old, "She was put in a hot tub." "SSSShhh," said the mother, and looking at me she said, "That happened a long time ago and the kids have all but forgotten."

Unfortunately, Lannie's mother could not face the past tragedy and help her daughter resolve the difficulties which appeared to have resulted from its impact. The mother quickly absented herself from the health care center and avoided the staff's efforts to contact her.

It is ironic, but instructive, that we can sometimes assist a mother–child couple whose personalities are beset with many troubles, as in the case of Joshua, but fail to help a mother and child with the aftermath of a single unhappy experience, although, as in the case of Lannie, mother and child have so many personality strengths.

Chapter 13

Helping Children Cope with Death

Erna Furman

Many of us go through life for long periods without thinking about death. When it suddenly strikes very close to us, it comes as a shock, not only because it always represents a loss but also because we get the horrible feeling that, this could be me; this could happen to me, to my family, to my children, and friends. We have a tendency to deal with this fear by adopting one of two extreme attitudes. We may feel the impact as though the tragedy had really happened to us. We put ourselves in the shoes of the bereaved or of the dying and feel so overwhelmed and anxious that we are unable to extend ourselves appropriately to those who need our help. At the other extreme, we shield ourselves and behave as if the situation is not real, and that we do not want to hear, read, or talk about it. This reaction too prevents us from extending a helping hand because it keeps us from coming to terms with our own feelings. Often we waver from one extreme to the other until perhaps we reach a kind of middle ground where we are able to feel, there but for the grace of God go I; it is not me but it could be. When we arrive at this hard-to-reach point we begin to be able to think and feel with others and to help them as well as ourselves.

Many years ago at the Hanna Perkins Therapeutic Nursery School, within one year, two mothers of young children died, leaving their families as well as therapists, teachers, peers, and friends stunned. We had to cope with the immediate reality and struggle to come to terms with what had happened. But in the course of the next few years, we found that, without having sought cases of bereavement, we had in intensive treatment 23 children of all ages who had lost a parent through death. Each analyst who treated a bereaved child and worked with the family found it so difficult and painful that we turned to each other to share and learn together. We hoped that in this way we would be better able to understand and help our patients and, perhaps, formulate some thoughts that might be of general interest and serve to assist others (E. Furman, 1974).

It does not take the death of a parent, of course, to bring children to an encounter with death. Many grandparents, siblings, relatives, and pets die. There are also many daily events which bring children face to face with death, be it a passing funeral procession or a dead worm in the backyard. The worst bereavement is the death of a parent. It is a unique experience distinct from all other losses, such as divorce or separation, and distinct from other experiences with death. Many nursery school teachers may be fortunate enough never to have a pupil whose parent dies, but they are surely called upon to help with some less tragic bereavements and the many daily encounters with death (the ants a child steps on or the dead mouse someone brings for show and tell [Hoffman, 1974]).

Our bereaved children came to treatment with many different symptoms. Parental death is unique; it happens to unique people who respond in unique ways. Our patients most often responded in a disturbed, unhealthy fashion, sometimes at the time of the bereavements, sometimes not until many years later. But we were deeply impressed that some children only about 2 years of age, because of very optimal circumstances, could master their tragic loss. By contrast, we had much older patients who could not master it at all. I do not mean to imply that 2-year-olds master this stress more easily than older children; on the contrary, it is harder for them, and the effects of a bereavement last longer. I am not speaking of the degree of pain and anguish, but the ability to achieve ultimate mastery. To me that means that these children were upset, struggled, and suffered, but were able to mourn their parents and to progress in their development. The danger of parental bereavement does not lie in the formation of isolated symptoms or difficulties. The main danger is that it may arrest or distort a child's development toward becoming a fully functioning adult. Many of the factors involved touch upon the role of the teacher and offer an opportunity to develop in children those qualities which will enable them to master a future bereavement or to help them and their peers to cope with a current loss or minor encounter with death.

HELPING CHILDREN UNDERSTAND DEATH

The first crucial factor is children's ability to understand death in its concrete manifestations; that is, to understand that death means no life, no eating, no sleeping, no pain, no movement. Those children who at the time of bereavement already had a rather good grasp of the concrete facts of death had a much easier time. We found that children from toddler age on show interest in dead things. They find dead insects or birds. When they can tell that a sibling is different from a teddy bear, that one is animate and the other not, they can also begin to understand what *dead* means. For example, when the toddler plays with a dead fly and notes that it does not move, it helps to confirm the child's observation by using the word *dead* and explaining that the fly will never move again because it is dead. Most young children have not yet been helped to acquire this kind of basic concrete understanding of what *dead* means, how things die, and what we do with the corpse. It is much easier to acquire concrete understanding of death from insects or small animals, since they do not have great emotional significance for the child; this knowledge paves the way for later understanding of death in people.

McDonald (1963) studied the responses of the peers of our two bereaved Hanna Perkins Nursery School pupils. She found that children's first interest focused on what death is, and they could not direct themselves to the aspects of loss, empathy, or sympathy for a peer's loss until they could understand concretely what death means. McDonald also noted that each of the children's questions required a special effort of thoughtful awareness and listening by the teachers. Initially, and without knowing it, teachers closed their eyes and ears and implied, without words, that death was not a welcome topic. Once their attitude changed, the children's questions just poured out. It is very difficult for all of us to talk about death, even dead insects. Most of us were not helped in this respect when we were children so we tend not to help children or do not know how to help them. With special effort and by struggling to come to terms with questions about death ourselves, it is possible to overcome our difficulty to some extent.

SUPPORT FOR PARENTS

Parents usually do not mind when teachers talk at school about death as it relates to insects, worms, or even animals. Some teachers have found it helpful to meet with parents to discuss how such incidents are handled. Parents, perhaps even more than teachers, find it very difficult to talk with children about death, fearing that sooner or later the child will ask, "Will I die?" "Will you die?" We are frightened of the answers that we would rather not give. However, the eventual next step in children's understanding death is that of relating it to themselves and to those they love and need. A meeting with parents on this subject does sometimes help to bring such questions into the open and offers the teacher an opportunity to help the parents. Whether a teacher wishes to arrange such meetings depends on the teacher's relationship with the parent group and the extent to which both sides are ready to grapple with the subject of death.

When a child asks, "Can this happen to me or to my mommy?" the answer should take into account the child's sense of time. A parent is hesitant to say, "No, I won't die," because he or she eventually will die. Yet should the parent say, "Yes, I will die," the child understands this to mean tomorrow or next week. We find that a young child can best understand when the parent says, "No, I do not expect to die for a long, long time," stressing the *no*, and adding that he or she expects to enjoy the child as a grown-up and have many years of being a grandparent.

Parents usually also raise the question of spiritual answers to the question of death. Children before age 5 or 6 are incapable of abstract thinking and therefore unable to grasp religious or philosophical explanations. They usually distort them into concrete and often frightening concepts that have little to do with religion. I know some very religious parents who chose not to introduce religious explanations to their children under the age of 5 precisely because they knew these concepts would be distorted and might later interfere with the children's attitudes about religion. By contrast, doubting or unbelieving parents quite often use explanations that involve *heaven* and *God*. This happens because they have not thought matters through themselves and want to shield the child from something frightening. In shielding the child they only shield themselves and create confusion in the child. Something that is not really believed by the adult cannot come across as true or reassuring to the child.

In our experience the most understanding parents have given concrete explanations of death and burial. When, in response to what they had heard from others, the children asked, "What about heaven?" or "Does God take people away?" the parents replied, "Many people believe that. Many people believe other things too, and as you get older you will learn about them and will understand them better. Right now it is important that you understand how we all know when someone is dead."

The concrete facts of death are usually much less frightening to children than to adults. An anecdote about one of Barnes's (1964) patients illustrates this point. A father had struggled very hard to help his young children understand what *dead* meant and what being in a coffin meant because their mother had died. Some months later their grandfather died. As the father tried to tell his little girl that they would choose a nice box with a soft blanket inside so that grandfather would be very comfortable, the little girl interrupted him and said, "But daddy, if he is really dead then it doesn't matter about his being comfortable in the coffin." For that moment the child certainly had a better grasp than the father.

BEARING UNPLEASANT FEELINGS

Another factor which facilitates a child's mastery of bereavement is the ability to bear unpleasant feelings, particularly sadness and anger. Obviously, there is no way to anticipate the kind of feelings that come with a bereavement. Separations are very different from a loss through death, but there are some similarities. Separations, to a small extent, involve the same feelings of longing, sadness, and anger that we find in much greater intensity at a time of bereavement. Young children are able to bear these feelings to an incredible extent if they have been given appropriate help in developing this strength.

How does one help a child achieve such mastery? Basically there are two ways, one of which is to expose children only to bearable separations. When separations are too long they become unbearable and therefore not conducive to experiencing feelings. A very few hours of separation are bearable for a baby, perhaps half a day for a toddler, and at most a couple of days for a nursery school child. But it takes more than adjusting the lengths of separation. The second important step is the adults' willingness to help children recognize their feelings, express them appropriately, and cope with them. Before and after the separation this is the parents' task; during the separation the caregiving person can help.

It is often thought that children who do not react, do not make a fuss, or even enjoy the parents' absence, are well-adjusted, good children. To me, these children have not built appropriate mental muscles to bear unpleasant feelings. They shut themselves off from such feelings and therefore have no control of them. An excellent time to practice with children in building up the mental muscles for knowing and bearing unpleasant feelings is, of course, during entry to nursery school. At that time teachers can help parents understand that children who have no feelings, who react as though nothing has happened, or who immediately "love" the school, are children who are shut off from their feelings and in danger of stunting their emotional growth. Many mothers who do not welcome the child's unhappy or angry response to separation at the start of school would be very concerned if the child did not react feelingly to the loss of a loved person or readily preferred someone else in that person's stead. Yet how could a child acknowledge very intense feelings without previous help to cope with them in less threatening situations?

Coping with Bereavement

So far we have considered how difficult it is to talk about death even in terms of animals and insects, and how hard to bear loneliness, sadness, and anger in terms of brief separations. We know, of course, how much greater the hardship is when we have to think about and feel fully the total loss of a loved person. There is no easy way to cope with bereavement. There is no short cut, either for the bereaved or for those who help them. The goal of assisting bereaved persons is not to foreshorten their pain and anguish or our own, but to strive toward inner mastery. Even if we achieve it, it does not mean that we have come to terms with death once and for all. In order to be able to help we too have to empathize anew with each bereavement and struggle through it again.

I would like to turn now to what teachers can do, and often have done, when a child in the nursery school suffers the death of a parent, sibling, or close relative. I do not have any easy remedies to offer, and my suggestions are much more easily said than done, because pain and anxiety are an essential part of the task.

The teacher first of all questions whether she should mention the loss to the child. I have heard time and again about the fear of causing a child hardship by referring to his or her loss. Some years ago I met a boy whose father had died. His teacher had reported that the boy had no feelings about, or reaction to, the death of the father. When I saw this boy, said "Hello" and expressed my natural sympathy, he broke into tears at once. He cried for an hour and I had to see him a second time before he could begin to talk. I asked him later why he had never shown his feelings at school. The boy replied, "You know, that teacher was so mean! He never even bothered to come to me and say 'I am sorry your father died.' I would never show my feelings to that kind of guy." I suspect that this was not a mean teacher but that his reaction of silence built a barrier between the child and himself.

This and similar experiences have convinced me that the teacher has to take the first step by mentioning the loss and expressing sympathy in a way that implies that the thoughts and feelings about the death will be in everyone's mind for a long time, that she hopes the child will feel free to come to her, talk with her, or feel with her about it. In practice, some children will come to the teacher much more than others. However often they do or do not come, the teacher needs to empathize with each and every feeling that may arise and help children tolerate them. This means not falsifying feelings, not holding them back, not even pouring them out in order to be rid of them, but rather to recognize and contain them.

At opportune times the teacher can also help by talking with the child about the factual aspects of the bereavement—how the loved one died, where he or she is buried, and changes in the family setting and routine. I think it is equally important for the teacher to report to the parent what the child shows, thinks, or feels about this experience so that the parent can further help the child and perhaps be alerted to some aspect which has not yet been expressed at home.

In addition to work with the child, a second area in which the teacher can be helpful is with the parents or surviving parent. It is to be hoped that before a loss occurs, the teacher will have built the kind of relationship with the parent which will make it possible for him or her to inform the teacher as a friend, a special professional friend who has the parent's and child's welfare at heart. Then the parent will welcome talking with this teacher and perhaps accept some suggestions—how to tell the child about the death, how to talk it over with the child, whether to take the child to the funeral, what plans to make for the immediate future.

ASSISTING PARENTS

Adults with young children do not die uncomplicated deaths; the deaths are always untimely. This is also true about the death of siblings. It is most important that the child understand not only that the parent or sibling is dead, but also the cause of death. When these two things are not understood, when they are distorted or denied, it is impossible for the child even to begin mourning. I do not mean that the child should be overwhelmed with frightening details, but a teacher can help a parent to tell the child enough and in such a manner that the child can achieve a considerable amount of understanding.

Parents always want to know whether they should take the child to the funeral, and what they should say about it. We can only give an answer after we learn more about the specific situation. The child's attendance at the funeral will depend on the type of service, how the parent feels about it, how comfortable the parent is with the rites the family observes, and how able the parent is to extend himself or herself emotionally to the child during the funeral.

Many families are willing to adapt the services to the needs of all the family. Children often find an open casket difficult. They find long services difficult. If the funeral rites are not suitable for a young child or if the parent is unable to care effectively for the child during the services, it is better that the child remain at home with a familiar person and with the full verbal knowledge of what is happening during that time. I had a patient who was sent to the zoo on the day of her father's funeral in the hope that she would not have to be sad. This hope was not fulfilled, and the arrangement produced an almost insurmountable barrier within the child and between child and surviving parent. Mourning has to happen together, pain and anguish have to be shared, it is not fair to shut out the child.

When it comes to immediate plans for the future, the teacher can sometimes impress upon parents how very important it is for the child's sake to keep the home and remaining family together. Adults often find it much easier to leave the place of distress, to throw away the things that remind them of the deceased. For children the opposite holds true. They need the concrete continuation and help of their surroundings in order to come to terms with what is missing. Sometimes people have asked how parents and children can ever be of support to one another when they have such different needs. When parents understand that their children's greatest need is continued physical and emotional care by the surviving parent, they usually compromise for the sake of the child and find that they benefit as well. Being a good parent brings a measure of self-esteem that cannot be gained in any other way and is especially helpful at a time of bereavement when so many other things seem not worthwhile.

HELPING OTHERS IN THE GROUP

Along with assisting the bereaved child and parent, the teacher has to extend help to the other children in the nursery school. This usually starts by discussing with the bereaved parent what to tell the other children and their families. It helps, of course, if the bereaved parent is able to share the truth in simple, realistic terms with his or her own child and is willing to have this information passed on. Then the teacher needs to take a few painful hours to call every parent in the nursery group. Each call is long and difficult and should, if possible, include several items: a brief account of what happened to their child's peer, which terms or phrases will be used in the nursery school to discuss the sad event, how the parents can tell their own child, and how helpful it would be if the child learned the news first from them, and how to cope with some of the child's questions.

If a bereaved parent is initially unable to allow discussion of the cause of death, the teacher may have to say, for example, "Chris's father died. It is still too hard for Chris's mommy to talk about it, but she will tell us what happened later and I will share it with you." If the teacher's relationship with the parent is a sound one, it will help to make this delay brief.

The next morning all children will have been told of the death, even if not its cause, by their parents, and the teacher can sit down with them and initiate the first discussion of facts and feelings. It is a most important point to emphasize that the first talk is only a beginning; that teacher and children will talk about it and feel about it often and for a long time; and that it will be with them all because it is a sad and scary thing.

There are usually three main questions that arise sooner or later: What is dead, can it happen to me, and can it happen to you? Until these questions are accepted and coped with, it is generally not possible for the peers or for their parents to extend genuine sympathy to the bereaved. When we are able to assist children in gaining gradual mastery, many months of painful struggle seem indeed worthwhile.

THE MOURNING PROCESS

If the death is understood, if its cause is understood, and the disposal of the body is understood, and if the bereaved child is reasonably sure of his own survival and of having bodily and emotional needs met to a sufficient extent, mourning will start of itself. It is a process that is not always visible from the outside because, contrary to what many people think, mourning does not consist of wailing, rages, crying, or complaining. Sometimes there are no overt signs of upset and yet the feelings may be there.

I worked with a mother and child. The little boy had lost his father two years previously and experienced some difficulty in the aftermath. The mother told me that she had never cried in front of the child, since she only cried when she was alone in bed. The boy, who supposedly had not reacted at all to his father's death and had certainly never cried or raged, told me in his separate interview that he was not a person who ever cried in front of people; he only cried when he was alone in bed and nobody knew that he cried; he cried night after night but his mother

never cried. Although mother and child expressed feelings in the same form, they did not know that the other
even had feelings. It was sad to see how hard they had
made it for themselves and for each other. However, even
if they had not cried at all they might have been able to
mourn because mourning is a mental process that consists primarily of two parts: on the one hand, a very gradual and painful detachment from the memories of the
deceased, and on the other hand almost the opposite, a
taking into oneself of some traits or qualities of the deceased. How much there is of each part and whether the
proportion leads to a healthy adaptive outcome depend
on many factors, including the age of the bereaved person,
the nature of the bereavement, the preceding relationship, the personality of the deceased. With young children
it is particularly important that they take into themselves the healthy rather than the sick attributes of the
dead parent and that they detach themselves sufficiently,
so that, in time, they will be free to form a parental bond
with a new person.

Sometimes parents intuitively understand the ways
in which their child's long inner mourning proceeds and
sense when the child encounters difficulties, but sometimes it is much harder. It certainly is not a mark of
failure to seek professional assistance at such a time, and
that is yet another area where the teacher can support
the surviving parent. The sooner help is given, the better
are the chances of preventing possible damage to the
child's growing personality.

Chapter 14

The Abused Child in the Nursery School

Erna Furman

Our Center's consulting work with preschool settings has increasingly included aggressively and sexually abused children. It is not an altogether new topic. Teachers have always brought some such cases for discussion and assistance. The recent increase probably does not reflect a higher incidence of either type of child abuse in the community but, more likely, indicates skilled and sensitive teachers' growing awareness of and ability to spot such difficulties. Child abuse is such a complex subject that we cannot aim to discuss it fully in this context. Indeed, we will not consider sexual abuse at all at this time because it is a quite separate pathology. Its effect on the child and related manifestations in his behavior, the involvement of the parents, and the role of the teacher differ markedly from those in cases of aggressive abuse. Even in regard to aggressive abuse we will address only the two issues which are usually of greatest concern to preschool educators: How can the teacher find out that a pupil has been abused, and what the teacher can and should do about it.

To start with, it is helpful for administrators and teachers to know and understand the law of their state regarding child abuse, and their own responsibility, if any, of reporting such cases. In many instances it is not an easy task even to interpret correctly the legal definition of abuse, and it may be much harder yet to apply it in specific instances, but familiarity with the law and a chance to consider its implications before we have to deal with a difficult practical situation, serve us as a useful preparation. For example, according to the Ohio Statute (Rev. Code Ann. 2151.42.1) we must consider "any wound, injury, disability, or condition of such a nature as to reasonably indicate abuse or neglect of such child." This covers a large number of conditions which may be viewed and interpreted differently by different people. An accurate assessment is made especially difficult by the fact that it is often hard to draw the line between child rearing practices and abuse. A necessary and legitimate means of discipline to one may be a form of abuse to another. Attitudes to physical punishment illustrate this. Parents often ask nursery school teachers to spank their children and even criticize preschools for refraining from physical punishment. Indeed, one of the teacher's first tasks with parent and child frequently focuses on clarifying such differences between home and school rules and assuring them that the nursery will provide order and safety without paddling. Likewise, it may be difficult to pinpoint exactly when parental handling constitutes neglect or significant mental and bodily harm.

For the teacher, however, the greatest difficulty does not lie in social and cultural variations of educational practices or in the purposeful vagueness of the law. Instead, it stems from the fact that the most serious cases of child abuse go most easily unnoticed because the parents and the child hide them. When parents tell us that they spanked or hurt their child, or when the child reproachfully tells on the parents, we should of course pay close attention and follow up on what may be a confession and call for help. It is not likely, however, that such instances betray severe or habitual abuse. The most dangerously abusive parents rarely let on about their behavior to the teacher, and it is extremely rare for their abused child to let an outsider know, in word or behavior, that the parents maltreat him or her. As a rule, such children do not complain of their injuries, do not exhibit them, do not speak of being angry at their parents or hating them, and do not usually act abusively in the nursery school. They often welcome the parent's arrival at the end of the school day and do not protest against going home. They are, not uncommonly, among the most conforming and quiet pupils, though perhaps lacking in emotional spontaneity.

Although the abusive parent's silence and evasiveness do not surprise us, the child's behavior is more puzzling. Yet there are many good reasons within the child's own personality and in his relationship with the parents to account for this conscious and unconscious secrecy. It is not only a question of fear. From among many reasons, let us mention at least a few. There is the fact that even abusive parents are needed and have to be seen as "good" to serve as an assurance to the child of his own survival and to remain a source for his self-esteem. Abusive parents are also loved for the emotionally healthy periods of care and kindness they often provide, but sometimes loved too for the episodes of abuse which may represent times of intense and exciting, albeit pathological, emotional closeness. Many youngsters actually get to enjoy being abused and "ask for it." They may also provoke the parents' mishandling to control it, to bring it about actively in preference to being passively surprised by it. This, as well as the parents' tendency to shift their guilt onto the child ("You had it coming to you"), often leads to the child's willingness to shoulder the blame. By hiding any signs of abuse the child protects the parent he has to idealize, protects himself from the parent, but also shields his own "badness" from the view of others—"If they find out I was beaten, they'll find out how bad I was."

HOW THEN CAN THE TEACHER FIND OUT ABOUT ABUSE?

With the cases in my consultation group, evidence of abuse sometimes came through chance observations. One teacher noticed a mark on a boy's back when his shirt was accidentally pulled up during climbing. The child did not reply to questions about it, but the teacher, now alerted, began to keep a closer eye on subsequent signs of injury, on the child–parent interaction, and on parental reports. In another case parental abuse first came to the teacher's attention when an instance was witnessed by other parents and children in the nursery school parking lot—a most unfortunate incident because it affected all the bystanders. In yet another case the mother told the teacher about her husband's abuse of her and the child. She did this in a moment of crisis, many months after the child had entered the school, but she refused to take action out of fear. Had the teacher not been available that day late in the afternoon, more months might have passed without it being mentioned.

More often, however, the teacher learns about child abuse much more indirectly. For example, throughout the year of a little girl's attendance at the day care center, the mother had harshly and persistently criticized the

teachers for inadequate care of her daughter and blamed
them for the many bruises her child allegedly sustained
at school. The bruises were there and the teachers, ever
more guilty and concerned, knocked themselves out to
keep an eye on Janie. She often played under tables or
in corners, so they worried that these were perhaps the
periods when she got injured, and they interceded and
protected her to the best of their ability. All was to no
avail, new and more hurts were ever present. Fortunately, the staff had, in spite of provocation and criticism,
built a fairly good working relationship with the mother.
This made it possible finally to wonder with her whether
she had similar difficulties with Janie at home and this,
in turn, led to the mother's confession that she was the
cause of all the bruises. She had placed the blame on the
school for fear of being found out and had attacked the
staff as she assumed they would criticize her if they knew.
In another case, the only overt sign of difficulty was the
child's and parent's inability to relate to the teacher and
their silent reticence in response to even the most innoc-
uous questions on any topic. The child was at school in
body but not in feeling; the mother came dutifully to all
conferences but could not reveal herself as a person. Real
contact was impossible. It took a long time, much thinking and putting together of little clues to realize that the
mother had earlier been reported for child abuse, and had
in fact been referred to the nursery after brief contacts
with the authorities. When her concern over being "found
out" could be appreciated, the mother's and child's difficulties could begin to be approached and worked on.

Persistent criticism of the school, avoidance of contacts and conferences with the staff, evasiveness about
the child's history and family life, and extreme touchiness
about questions relating to it, are not infrequent signs
of parental difficulty with abuse, but they are by no

means the only ways in which child abuse can come to the teacher's attention. The examples merely afford a glimpse of how aware, knowledgeable, and tactful a teacher needs to be to learn about these situations. It is very important to remember that child abuse does not occur only among the poor or deprived, indeed, no setting is exempt. We have seen as many cases in private half-day nurseries in affluent suburbs as from day care centers in the city ghettos. All teachers need to be aware of the possibility that a pupil may be an abused child and they need to be alert to the fact that evidence of abuse may reach them in a very unexpected and roundabout fashion.

ONCE THE TEACHER DOES KNOW OF ABUSE, WHAT DOES SHE HAVE TO DO AND HOW CAN SHE DO IT TO BEST BENEFIT THE CHILD AND FAMILY?

In each instance the teacher faces a professional and human responsibility, but she may also have a legal responsibility. For example, according to Ohio law, a schoolteacher and school authority are among the professionals specifically responsible for reporting to the local peace officer incidents of known abuse or neglect and situations where there is reason to believe that it has occurred. The penalty for failure to report is a fine and/or imprisonment. Experience has shown that it is very difficult for teachers to meet these responsibilities. In many cases, the parents' mere inkling that the teacher has come to know of their abuse, leads to a lot of hard feelings and to the immediate withdrawal of the child from the nursery. This happens especially frequently when the school notifies the authorities, regardless of whether the school informed the parents before or immediately after filing the report, and even when the school chose to report anonymously, in which case the family suspected or quickly traced the source. In some such instances the family "disappeared" altogether and could not be located by the authorities. Even when the officials could make contact, the parents were defensive and angry, and failed to cooperate effectively with those assigned to help them. Also, the personality difficulties which cause parents to abuse their children, tend to affect their behavior toward others. Touchy to criticism, they readily "turn the tables" on the staff who knew of, and perhaps reported, their offense. Some such parents riled up other parents and agencies in the community against the school with false accusations. Some nursery school teachers were personally threatened and harassed, were even endangered in their homes, and required police protection.

Since one can never be sure of avoiding such unhappy consequences, a teacher should not attempt to deal with the situation on her own. As soon as a teacher gets to know of a case of child abuse or even suspects there may be one, it is mandatory for her to share this information with the director and the director, in turn, needs to inform her board or supervisor, so that a decision on the best way to proceed is taken with the knowledge and consent of those ultimately responsible for matters concerning the school. It is also advisable for every preschool or center to have access to legal consultation to assure that any steps taken are in keeping with the requirements of the law. No teacher or director, however skilled and well intentioned, should keep just to herself knowledge of abuse, nor should she arrive independently at a decision as to how to proceed in regard to it; doing so could implicate the teacher legally. It could also place an undue burden of personal and professional responsibility on her shoulders. It is often difficult to gauge how dangerous the abuse may be, how quickly it could become worse, and which are the most suitable measures of assistance and protection in a given case. Although the teacher often knows a good deal about a family and enjoys their trust, she is not in a position to assess their situation adequately. It is therefore often helpful to consult also with a psychiatrist or mental health professional. This does not mean that the teacher should not be involved in the discussion and handling of the situation. On the contrary, in instances where events have taken a more fortunate turn it was usually the teacher's relationship with the parents which made it possible to convince them of the school's good will and wish to continue work with them, although the law could not be sidestepped.

Obviously, the school's decision on how to proceed needs to take into account many factors. When the law strictly requires direct reporting to the state appointed agency or officer and when the child appears to be in immediate serious danger, we have no choice. In these situations we run the greatest risk of alienating the parents and of being unable to help them toward working on their problem. But this is not always the inevitable outcome. For example, in some such instances we suddenly learn that the parent is a known offender, worked with the agency of protective service before, and is quite willing to resume work in connection with the current repeat of abuse. Such parents are sometimes relieved by the school's knowledge and constructive, nonjudgmental attitude, and are glad to keep the child at the school.

With some cases of child abuse, the teacher may feel that she could help a parent better toward recognizing the problem and working on it if she did not report directly to the state authorities but utilized her relationship with the parents to refer them for competent assistance to a social agency, medical facility, or community service which would then assume the responsibility for the case.

Such referrals are most effective when the teacher knows the agency and its way of working and, especially, when she can give the parent a specific name of a professional she respects and trusts. Handling the matter by means of referral has many advantages. It minimizes the threat to the parents, supports the part of them that wants to improve their handling of the child, gives their involvement with a helping professional a better chance, and makes it possible for the school to keep the child and to do their part in assisting him and his family. The personality problems connected with abuse, for parent and child, are most complex, difficult to work with, and invariably take a long time to resolve. Any measure of willing effort, trust, and cooperation on the parent's part is most helpful. A sufficiently positive relationship with the teacher therefore counts a great deal at the time of initial referral and during the parent's subsequent work on his or her problem. In many geographical areas the Welfare Department, by law in charge of cases of child abuse, is well aware of all this as well as of its own usually limited facilities. For these reasons it often does not administer the law in such a way as to require direct reporting in all instances, but supports the help parents get from other professional services and allows schools to meet their legal responsibility by referring cases to recognized agencies, groups, or individuals. In a number of cases, referral by the school has worked out well, averted possible danger, and contributed to the parents' ability to work toward improvement.

At best, each instance of child abuse presents a difficult problem for a school to deal with; there are no easy solutions. However, if we are prepared, we are usually better able to work out solutions as sensibly as possible. It helps to be cognizant, in advance, of our responsibilities and of the steps that should be taken to meet them. It also helps us to prepare ourselves emotionally, to come to terms with the shocking realization that one of our very own pupils could be a victim of abuse, and to acknowledge that his or her abusive parents are not monsters but people, albeit people with deep-seated serious problems. Such an awareness will enable us to undertake the stressful task of assisting them with a realistic, calm and tactful attitude.

Chapter 15

Readiness for Kindergarten

Erna Furman

In my own experience and that of others, the topic of readiness for kindergarten crops up not long after the Christmas vacation when either a child or a parent mentions public school for the first time. We usually respond with a jolt, realizing that the last half of the nursery year is upon us and that we shall be laboring under the increasingly pressing prospect of kindergarten—or should I say "dread" of kindergarten? In truth, the idea of entering public school is apt to make parents, children, and teachers a bit anxious. The step implies showing oneself to the world, letting society judge whether one amounts to something. The children worry whether they will be adequate to the demands of the "big" school; the parents worry how their child's behavior will reflect on their parenting; and we teachers too feel that we are supposed to have contributed to the child's readiness and advised the parents on his ability to cope with kindergarten, so that the little boy's or girl's performance in public school will show how competent we are as educators.

When people are anxious, they are not very rational. For this reason the topic of kindergarten readiness tends

to become beclouded with tensions and misunderstandings, while common sense may recede into the background. Of course, the feelings and worries we have about
kindergarten, as teachers, parents, or children, are important to understand and to deal with. In the second half
of this article we shall specifically look at these emotional
concerns and see how we can best help parents, children,
and ourselves to come to terms with them. First, however,
I should like to focus on the knowledge, skills, and personality attributes that constitute kindergarten readiness in a child. We shall be in a better position to cope
with our own and others' feelings when we have these
objective facts at our fingertips.

SOME PERSONALITY ACHIEVEMENTS THAT INDICATE READINESS FOR KINDERGARTEN

Many parents focus on specific aspects of academic
readiness (Does he know his colors and letters? How far
can he count? Is he beginning to read?), and on certain
motor skills (Can he use scissors, skip, tie his shoes?), in
the hope that the child's achievements in these areas will
allay their broader, often unexpressed, concerns as to
whether the child will be a good learner. Will he be socially accepted and accepting? Will he be able to utilize
the school to grow and mature? Teachers, like parents,
put some store by individual academic or motor skills,
but are usually also more concerned about other characteristics. These are often quite easy to pinpoint in specific situations; for example, Johnny can read a bit but
cannot sit still in a story group; Jane is very good at
skipping and zipping but has wetting accidents. We know
that not being able to sit still or wetting one's pants will
handicap a child in kindergarten. We readily single out
such striking individual difficulties. It is harder to put

one's finger on subtler interferences and developmental lags, and harder yet to assess their significance within the total framework of the child's personality.

Over the years much thought has been devoted to pinpointing and understanding which attributes a child has to have and which developmental steps he needs to have mastered in order to function at the age-appropriate level that qualifies him as ready for kindergarten (E. Furman, 1969b; Steininger and Krueger, 1971). The present discussion includes and builds on the ideas we have formulated, but it still does not cover all aspects of kindergarten readiness and its conclusions are far from final.

Some developmental masteries necessary for kindergarten readiness are not very different from the prerequisites for starting nursery school which we reviewed in talking about the roles of parents and teachers (Chapter 1). Among these is *the ability to grapple with, and master, new experiences.* Let me explain this by taking as an example the different ways in which children cope with orienting themselves in a new nursery school. Some children pester their mothers for weeks before entry with their many questions about school, with their protests and complaints of what they will not like, with requests to drive by the building, or to peek into the windows or playground. When they finally begin to attend, their eyes drink in every detail of the new setting. At times they blurt out critical comments which reveal their efforts to compare the familiar with the strange: "Those toilets are too little"; "It's silly to hang your jacket in a cubby"; "It smells funny in here." They know quite soon where the bathroom is, where the food is prepared, by which door one leaves. It does not take them much longer to locate the various toys and to anticipate the sequence of routines. By contrast, other children show no active interest in advance. Sometimes they do not even listen to the mother's attempts at preparing them. When they enter they look lost, wander around aimlessly, or rush around from one toy to the next without really playing with any of them. The teacher's explanations appear to go in one ear and out the other. Many days, even weeks, go by before they can be relied upon to know which door is used to reach the playground, where the toilets are, where their coats belong, which activity follows which. They seem generally uneasy, bewildered, but do not voice specific criticisms.

The former children anticipate the new experience and utilize available preparation. When confronted with the unknown they link it to the known by noting similarities and differences, thus gaining mental mastery of the new setting. Basically, their attitude is illustrative of how all learning proceeds: preparing oneself for the task, building on the familiar, and picking out the new, putting old and new together, and making them one's own. In this way what is newly learned fits into an increasingly sophisticated mental framework and forms the base for progressing to more advanced tasks.

The bewildered "lost" children panic at the new experience instead of coming to grips with it. They confront it without inner preparation and cannot bring their knowledge of the familiar to bear on it. Each new piece of learning disorients and overwhelms them because they have to start from scratch. Even when they finally come to terms with it, the newly learned is not assimilated into a coherent context which will make it possible to tackle more difficult experiences in the future.

A teacher is in a good position to assess this area of readiness. There are many opportunities to observe how a child responds to preparation for the unusual school event (an outing, a change in routine, a visitor, new play material), how he manages these situations, and whether he can utilize the teacher's assistance in gaining mastery.

The second area of readiness is also one which we already look for to some extent at the start of nursery school: *bodily independence* and an ability to care for one's belongings. This includes self-feeding with appropriate use of some implements and being independent in toileting without relying on adult reminders or assistance. It also implies an ability to care for one's bodily well-being: to avoid common dangers, to defend oneself appropriately, to recognize and differentiate discomforts, such as feeling tired, hungry, or ill, and if necessary to request adult help, for example when one has sustained an injury or does not feel well. Knowing the names for different body parts is not necessarily related to this. In normal development the child who is cognizant of his bodily sensations is usually also interested in learning the names of the body parts. As he achieves the kindergarten level he is then able to state specifically, "My ear hurts" or "My throat is sore." He does not become irritable without relating it to the real cause nor does he complain in a more infantile way, "I don't feel good" or "My tummy hurts" (the young child's tummy usually being the equivalent of his whole body). The important thing, however, is that he knows *when* he hurts and what to do about it, rather than that he be able to name his body parts.

Care of one's clothes and belongings is an integral part of this area and can be observed readily at nursery school. When a mother recently described how unready her boy was in his first nursery, she illustrated it perceptively by saying, "When it was time to go out, Jim not only could not put *on* his jacket, he didn't even know which one *was* his jacket." It is similar with children's attitudes to their belongings. A child who is "with it" knows what he has brought from home, keeps an appropriate (I do not mean excessive and anxious) eye on the toy or object, or requests the teacher's help in taking good care of it. By contrast some children as yet hardly recognize their own toys, leave them around, forget about them, and expect the adults to care for them. This ability to extend one's liking of and caring for oneself to clothes and possessions differs from having the skill to manipulate them—to zip and unzip, to fasten buttons, to tie laces. Usually children who have made their things their own also want to do for themselves and work toward increasing bodily independence. A child may be a little clumsy and take longer to master each task, but that is not a detriment as long as he is motivated and applies himself toward reaching the goal. The mere acquisition of isolated skills, however, even if well performed, such as tying shoelaces, is not indicative of kindergarten readiness unless the child views them in the wider context of wanting to care for himself.

The third area is the child's ability to form and maintain a *teacher–pupil relationship*. This developmental step is crucial to all later learning, from kindergarten on, and therefore is one of the main tasks a child needs to master during his nursery school years. We defined the teacher–pupil relationship in Chapter 1 as being the first relationship a child makes which serves a specific function, in this instance the function of learning with and from a person whose job it is to teach him. Prior to about age 3 the child maintains primarily a relationship with his mother, or mothering person, which includes all functions and satisfies all of the child's needs. Up to that time too, the child's other relationships, within and without the family, are either additions to the mother–child relationship or substitutes for it.

How can we tell when a child has formed an appropriate relationship with us as teachers? One sign is the child's ability to differentiate parent and teacher, home and school. He appreciates and conforms to certain differences between them—differences in rules, in behavioral expectations, in the type of activities and material, in traditions, such as how stories are read and how birthdays are celebrated. Another is the manner in which the child bridges the gap between home and school. Is he able to share with the teacher some of what happens at home and with the mother what happens at school? Does he share appropriately? For example, does he bring his new toy to show, acorns for the science table, an account of a building going up nearby? Or does he share inappropriately, for example, by bringing his baby blanket, or an object from home that nobody should touch, or a garbled account of his night fears? Another indication of readiness is that the child behaves better at school than at home. Mothers often misinterpret this differentiation and worry that the teacher handles the child better than they do and that he therefore "behaves better for them." Actually it takes a lot of good mothering to enable a child to form a relationship with a teacher and to enjoy a school setting. This enjoyment of the opportunities for learning within the context of the relationship with the teacher is in itself an important sign. It differs from the child who feels close to the teacher but demands the wrong returns—physical affection and care, exclusive attention, involvement in instinctual conflicts and gratifications.

The fourth area is *relationships with peers.* We hope that by the time a child gets ready for kindergarten he has the ability to engage in a give-and-take relationship with other children in structured activities (where one has to take turns and conform to rules) as well as in fantasy play (where one has to take complementary roles and compromise on one's ideas in order to work out a mutually satisfactory participation).

We also hope that peer relations will show some beginnings, at least now and then, of a true friendship. By
this I mean a bond which is based on an appreciation of
each other's feelings and which includes concern and com-
passion for each other as well as the wish to make one's
friend happy. This is a major developmental step and
many children do not take it till the end of kindergarten.
Before that time we more often observe the ways in which
the 4- and 5-year-old's family conflicts interfere in his
friendships. When he feels much too little and incompe-
tent in comparing himself to his parents, he turns the
tables on his peers and, by bossing, boasting, or belittling,
attempts to be one up on *them*. When he feels painfully
left out of some aspects of the relationship between
mother and father, he tends to make others feel jealous
by using the "two is company, three is a crowd" method.
It is an indication of healthy development when these
interferences are not all-pervasive but leave some room
for making a real friend. In addition, we now expect at
least some ability to observe and cope with the ways in
which other children are different from himself. Such
differences may be of a physical nature (racial or ethnic
characteristics, clothing styles, minor or major deformities), or of a behavioral nature (shyness, aggressiveness,
manners, idiosyncracies, problems in adjustment). It is
a mark of a kindergartener's age-appropriate self-esteem
as well as of his having been helped adequately in dealing
with others, when he can observe such facts, figure them
out or ask about them, try to understand and accept them,
and adapt his own behavior realistically to the "different"
child. In some instances this means staying away from
a child at potentially dangerous times or preparing for
proper self-defense (e.g., an unpredictably aggressive
child); in others it means appreciating that the difference
is unfortunate for the child but does not pose a real threat

to others (e.g., a child with a deformity, idiosyncracy, or emotional difficulty); and in others yet it means knowing that physical or cultural differences (e.g., racial or ethnic differences) are not shortcomings either in the other person or in oneself.

In kindergarten—in the classroom, at recess time, in the playground before and after school, and on the walk to and from school—it is helpful to understand others in this way in order to know whom to befriend and whom to guard against. In the absence of this ability for realistic judgment, children tend to feel threatened by *all* differences which, depending on their individual ways of coping with fear, may lead them to avoid the harmless, provoke the aggressive, tease and hurt the feelings of the unfortunate, or imitate the troubles of others.

The fifth area of readiness concerns *play*, more specifically those forms of play which pave the way for the transition to work (A. Freud, 1963); play with toys, in contrast to the more primitive play with the body (compare the child who strokes his hair and cuddles his blanket with the child who practices climbing). It is also play that is in the service of role taking or of skill acquisition, in contrast to the earlier play which brings instinctual pleasures (compare the child who is earnestly absorbed in producing a picture at the easel with the one who excitedly uses the paints and brush to make a mess). The difference is not necessarily evidenced by the quality of the end product (even a dedicated young painter may not achieve a representational or neat picture!) but by the expression on the child's face and by the nature of his body movements. In fact, most teachers knowingly take the excited face and jerky wild motions as a sign of incipient trouble and suggest clean-up or a calmer activity.

This brings us to the other characteristics of the more mature, kindergarten-ready play, namely the child's pleasure in the process of making something and in the end result he has achieved. Enjoyment of the process and of the outcome do not necessarily go together. A child who delights in painting may not treasure the picture he produced. He does not show it to others, does not take care of it, or take it home. Another child may not especially enjoy painting but endures it long enough for the sake of completing the picture. It is joyfully held high for all to see, carefully stored in the cubby, and proudly handed to mother at going home time. Ideally, the child who is ready for kindergarten will have acquired a taste for some enjoyment of the process, and some enjoyment of the end product, because experiencing these rather advanced pleasures motivates him to work toward reexperiencing them and enables him to muster the effort it takes to do so.

The last but by no means least area of readiness relates closely to the capacity for working: *inner controls*. These enable the child to deal with his needs, urges, and feelings in such a way that he wants to, and can, coordinate them with the demands of reality and of the moral and cultural values of his milieu instead of expressing them directly and attaining immediate unmodified gratification. In other words, when a child has achieved a measure of inner controls he complies, to a considerable extent, with the three basic dicta of education, not this but that, not here but there, not now but later, and begins to function as a "civilized" member of his small community. He can wait a while for his meal even when he is hungry; he can use the bathroom in anticipation of a longer shopping trip; he can take turns at a game even when he very much wants to be first; he can accept an alternate toy when the one he wants is unavailable; he can work at a hard puzzle without giving up, and can postpone the pleasure of success. He can forego a desired activity because the school schedule demands that he get ready to go home. In these and many other ways he demonstrates that he can modify his wishes, accept substitute pleasures, bear frustration, and delay gratification.

A number of factors combine to make this momentous development of inner controls possible. Two of them stand out as the most significant—speech and the emergence of conscience.

As to speech I do not mean simply the knowledge of vocabulary and the ability to talk clearly and coherently, but the use of speech for meaningful communication of thoughts and feelings (Katan, 1961; Kirst, 1976). This includes being able to listen to the verbalized thoughts and feelings of others because communication is a mutual process. It also presupposes the child's ability to recognize within himself his ideas, needs, and feelings and to know the right words for them. When a child is able to recognize what he feels—anger, happiness, jealousy, or loneliness—and when he knows each feeling by name, he takes a big step toward internal mastery over the feeling. Instead of experiencing a vague multitude of sensations which press for behavioral discharge, he is able to organize his sensations into a specific symbolic entity, a word, which helps him to contain and tolerate the feeling and to express it verbally instead of in action. It is sometimes mistakenly assumed that children should be encouraged to "say the feeling" in order to "get rid" of it. Actually, verbalizing feelings provides but limited gratification and discharge. Its main purpose is to give the child a mental tool for inner mastery and control, for thought in lieu of action. When John *knows* he is mad because Jim has a new toy, he need not snatch away the toy, or hit Jim, or sulk in the corner, but can tolerate his anger and perhaps say, "I don't like it when people get new toys" or "I'm mad that he got a new toy." Having mastered the feeling he is then freer to think out a possible solution, such as, "May I play with it for a while?" or "I'll let you play with my toy if you let me play with yours."

The ability to recognize and tolerate feelings also plays a part in conscience formation, the second main factor contributing to inner controls. The child about to enter kindergarten is expected to have acquired a set of ideals for himself that reflect basic realistic educational demands; for example, liking to be clean rather than dirty, kindly behaved rather than mean, patient rather than impatient. In practice this is evidenced by an awareness of increased self-esteem when the child has lived up to his ideals ("Look how clean I washed my hands!" "I was *real* kind to Lisa, I gave her one of my candies!") and by feeling bad when he has let himself down. The latter may lead to a wish to make amends, either in the form of an apology or of repairing the damage (taping a torn book, cleaning up the mess). Most of all we look for evidence that the child anticipates feeling bad when he is about to do something wrong and can use this inner reminder to stop himself. Sometimes even the child's ability to heed the teacher's reminder is a step in that direction, "John, remember how bad you felt when you didn't pick up the blocks the other day? Better get it done quickly so this time you'll be pleased with yourself." It is not an indication of conscience when the child *only* hopes to avoid the authority's wrath for wrongdoing. Sometimes, however, pleasing others and pleasing himself go together; for example, when the child reports "Look how clean I washed my hands!" his satisfaction with himself is confirmed and augmented by the teacher's approval of him.

These personality achievements are our basic criteria for assessing a child's readiness for kindergarten. The majority of youngsters qualify fairly adequately. Among those who do not, it is the rare 5-year-old who lags in all areas. More often a child functions appropriately in some respects, inappropriately in others. It is a common mistake to attribute these lags and deviations to "immaturity" and to assume that time—especially in the form of an extra year in nursery school—will enable the child to "catch up." Age-appropriate development is only in part determined by an inherent maturational timetable. A plant's growth potential is released by its nourishing medium. Similarly, the child's maturational progress interacts at all times with his facilitating environment—his family, his school, and all the helpful and unhelpful experiences life puts in his path. Each of the areas we listed is individually achieved by a fortuitous combination of all these factors. A serious defect in physical or mental endowment cannot be fully compensated for by the best educational assistance; environmental interferences or lacks can, in turn, stunt a child's maturational progress or cause it to deviate along pathological lines.

When do we begin to assess kindergarten readiness? How can we understand the causes of difficulties? What measures do we take to correct them? When can a child profit from an additional year of nursery school? How do we share our knowledge and recommendations with the child and parents? These are hard questions each nursery school teacher has to face. We shall return to them at the conclusion of this chapter, after we have looked more closely at the feelings related to kindergarten entry and how to cope with them.

FEELINGS RELATED TO KINDERGARTEN ENTRY

At the beginning I mentioned one of the important feelings that teachers, parents, and children share in re-

gard to the prospect of kindergarten, namely, "How will
I show up? What will they think of me? Which shortcomings will be revealed and which criticisms leveled at me?"

The second main feeling that all three parties share
is the concern about the separation from the loved and
the familiar which is inevitably entailed in the transition
to kindergarten. For the teacher the child's leaving constitutes a physical and mental loss. Sometimes the
teacher may be quite glad to be rid of a pupil, but usually
she has invested herself in working with a child for one
or two years and will keenly miss him. The teacher knows
that the successful nursery school graduate does not come
back, that it is in the nature of growing up for him to
hold his elementary school teacher in high esteem and
to forget, or look down a bit, on the baby school he left
behind. Even if he does return for a visit or we meet him
by chance, he no longer responds to us in terms of the old
relationship. It is a real loss and engenders strong feelings, especially because we have to go through this experience so many times.

The mother also feels a loss but of a different kind.
She will still see her child daily, perhaps even for the
same number of hours, so she is not so much affected by
the physical separation. Hers is a more poignant separation: a change in the child which is accompanied by an
inevitable change in the mother–child relationship.
Mothers have an inkling that the child's entry into public
school coincides more or less with a big developmental
step. The unique emotional closeness with the mother,
so characteristic of the preschool years, gives way to a
relative withdrawal. While the schoolchild can get along
well with his parents and share with them his interests
and activities, he will never again relate to them in the
exclusive, mutually empathic way of the younger child.
Increasingly, the parents will not know intuitively what

he thinks and feels, will not even know what he experiences. People outside his family will, in many respects, seem more important to him than members of the family. "My teacher said" will rank above what mother and father say, in contrast to the underfive for whom the parent's word is always the last. The child forges ahead, the parents are left behind. Of course mothers have faced the child's growing away before—when he started nursery school, when he learned to love his teacher, when he changed from a toddler whose relationship revolved around bodily care to a preschooler who needed his mother to think, feel, and talk with him. But these previous steps did not diminish the basic mother–child closeness. The step into the school age phase does just that. It is very difficult for mothers because they usually know only vaguely what they are going through and because they tend to chide themselves for not rejoicing wholeheartedly at their children's growing up.

The children too experience losses. They have to say good-bye to their nursery school and teacher whom they know and love, and they sense that they are about to change in their relationship with their parents. However, compared to teachers and parents, their concerns over separation are paralleled by a strong maturational wish to leave the old behind and to experience new things. So whereas the parent, and to some extent the teacher, bemoans the loss of something that was wonderful and is never going to happen again, the child looks forward to better things to come. As one perceptive youngster remarked to his mother, "You will miss me more than I'll miss you, because you're in the middle of your life but I'm at the beginning."

We do not have the choice of having or not having feelings, they are a natural part of our makeup, but we have some control over the role they will play in our thinking and actions. When we are aware of our own feelings we are better able to master them in ourselves and to appreciate and empathize with them in others, and this in turn makes it possible to understand and help people. When we are not fully cognizant of our own feelings they tend to obscure our rational judgments, affect our behavior adversely, and blind us to the manifestations of feelings in others. As a result we may end up at cross-purposes with the very people we wish to help. The nursery school teacher's task, however, goes beyond having to recognize her own feelings and empathize with parents and children. She also often has to assist them in becoming aware of their feelings and coping with them so that parents and children too will be able to look at entry to kindergarten realistically and so that their actions will be less burdened by emotional concerns. How can one approach this task with children and parents?

Children's feelings come to the fore most clearly and can be talked about most appropriately during the long process of preparation for kindergarten which starts several months prior to the end of nursery school. At first teachers usually introduce a number of academic activities geared to kindergarten readiness (writing one's name, worksheets for number concepts and reading skills). At a later point, many nursery schools practice procedures that are specific to their neighborhood kindergartens (a bell ringing to mark certain times, the pledge of allegiance to the flag, lining up to go to the playground, raising one's hand to speak). Some nursery schools are also able to arrange for their groups of "prekinders" trial rides in the school bus, visits to the public school playground and classroom, meetings with the kindergarten teacher in the nursery school. From the start it helps to tell the children with each step that this activity is going to make them feel comfortable in the kindergarten and will help them know that they can really do there what will be expected of them. Most important, however, we add that the activity will give them a chance to talk about the things they like or do not like about going to kindergarten. The factual preparation indeed is not an end in itself nor is it intended to eliminate unhappy feelings. Rather, the preparatory activities are opportunities to experience and cope with feelings as we talk about them before, during, and after each activity. The more ways we can devise to acquaint the children with the realities of the kindergarten and the more they are able to familiarize themselves with the unknown, the better can they focus their questions and concerns and the better can we help them to correct misunderstandings, fantasies, or misconceptions and to recognize and deal with their feelings.

Sometimes we are surprised at the directness of the children's responses and at the comfort they derive from our empathy—"Oh, I'll miss you, Miss T." "Of course, I'll miss you too, Jimmy, good-byes are always hard"; "That school has a scary playground." "Yes, it's always a bit scary when things are new. In time you will get to know it well and then it won't feel so scary." At other times the children's feelings are hidden from themselves and others and require gentle recognition by the teacher: Peter refuses to do his worksheets and the teacher finds time to ask him about it and to suggest they talk it over. Peter is unlikely to spill out his concerns there and then but within hours or days he may say something about kindergarten that will help to clarify his ideas for us. Yet at other times we find that the children are disappointed rather than reassured by finding out what is expected of them; for example, we sometimes learn that they looked upon entering kindergarten as an "instant grow-up" (in the words of one little girl) and hoped they would indeed at once read there like the grown-ups.

There is a lot to feel, a lot to sort out, and getting ready for kindergarten therefore takes a long time with many ups and downs. The teacher's help can be invaluable.

Let us now turn to the parents and how we can help them. Actually, the parents often bring up the issue of kindergarten before the children do. It may be in the form of a query about registration or a threat to the dawdling youngster, "You won't be allowed to do that in kindergarten!" Experience has shown that it is most helpful to use the first opportunity to mention what a difficult step kindergarten entry is because it brings with it such hard feelings. Sometimes the mother's comment can serve as an "in" to such a talk, or one can refer to it oneself. "Kindergarten is always a very difficult thing for me. When the kids go on to kindergarten I kind of lose them and I hate to see that happen. And yet I want nothing more than for them to do well and so of course I worry how they will make out. What will those public school teachers think of them and, for that matter, what will they think of the preparation I gave them? I know the children get worried about kindergarten too and that's very understandable. And many mothers have told me that it's a trying time for them too." One tries, from the start, to show empathy with the mother's feelings, to stress that she, her child, and the teacher share some of the feelings, and that it would be a mistake to talk about kindergarten readiness without taking feelings into account.

When we miss out on the chance to put the true feelings squarely in the forefront, they are, as I mentioned earlier, apt to enter into the discussion in a less helpful way. For example, it is quite common for an unrecognized fear of criticism to surface in the form of a critical attack on others. Thus, mothers who do not realize that they are worried how they and their children will show up, may become very critical of their child's performance (urging him to produce or catch up suddenly), or of the nursery school's program (it has not taught the children what they need to know), or of the public school (they do not know how to handle children). Unfortunately, the nursery school teacher may be drawn into the mother's attitudes. She may side with the mother in becoming impatient with the child's imperfections; she may respond to the mother's criticisms of the nursery by becoming defensive and unsympathetic; or she may join in the mother's criticisms of the public school and thereby jeopardize chances of a cooperative relationship with the kindergarten teacher. It is often forgotten that the latter feels just as threatened, worries whether she will be able to work well with a whole new group of youngsters, and fears the blame of parents and preschool teachers for "not handling the children well." She too can readily respond to "attacks" by disparaging the child, his home, or his previous school. In this way a shared feeling of apprehension and insecurity is replaced by a vicious cycle of mutual hostilities. Cooperation between kindergarten and home as well as between kindergarten and nursery school becomes impossible and the child bears the brunt as he finds himself the target or pawn of the adults' animosities instead of receiving their sympathy and support with his own worries. By contrast, when we help parents to recognize their own as well as the children's and teachers' feelings, such impasses can be avoided, working together can be promoted and it becomes easier for them to address themselves objectively to the issues of kindergarten readiness.

PARENTS NEED TO UNDERSTAND AND HELP
WITH KINDERGARTEN READINESS

Parents are not professional educators and cannot know everything about what kindergarten readiness consists of, how the nursery school curriculum prepares children for public school, or how they can help their children with this developmental step. It is the nursery school teacher's task to assist them by providing the appropriate information and, as with the children, to include in these discussions the feelings that inevitably accompany them.

Early group meetings with parents can be used to discuss the various prerequisites for kindergarten readiness. This forms a basis for parents and teachers to assess individual children with the same goals in mind. It also helps them to gauge the child's readiness, lags, or trouble areas in good time when home and school still have a chance to work with the child and assist him in progressing before the final decision on readiness has to be made. In one of our Center's consultation seminars, the teachers and I also worked out a written "Guideline for Child Observation and Evaluation" (Sabath, Eber, Hoffman, and Wagner, 1981) for this purpose. It lists the areas of personality functioning and specific achievements the teacher needs to observe and work on with each child and enables the parents to participate and follow their child's progress with the help of their copy of the same outline. During their periodic conferences, parents and teachers can then compare and discuss their respective evaluations and plan together how best to assist the child in mastering lags and difficulties. This joint endeavor is undertaken at the very start of the nursery school year, has been greatly appreciated by many parents, and has proved of benefit to their children.

Nursery schools also find it useful to inform parents,

individually or in groups, how the school curriculum assists children in developing the necessary prekindergarten skills. Many parents cannot, without help, understand a specific activity in terms of its component skills. For example, it is not uncommon for parents to criticize a field trip to the nearby grocery store as lacking in intellectual or cultural stimulation. They do not always appreciate that such a trip is not undertaken as an academic learning activity but as an exercise in areas of personality functioning which are requisite for kindergarten readiness. Can the child profit from the preparatory discussion and follow the outlined plan step by step, or is he unable to anticipate what is going to happen and reacts with bewilderment and surprise during the trip? Can he share the teacher sufficiently to walk comfortably with an assigned peer or does he have to hold the teacher's hand or make special demands on being first or last with this boy or that girl? Can he control his bodily needs or does he need a drink or a bathroom visit during the trip? Can he be content to buy the planned item and delay eating it until he returns to school, or does he have to touch and pick up articles on the shelves and demand to eat "just a little bit now"? With help, parents can learn to recognize the many accomplishments necessary for a successful grocery trip with the school and see how it differs from shopping with them.

When parents know what kindergarten readiness is about and when they understand how the nursery school assists the child's development in the respective areas, they can coordinate their own educational efforts with those of the school. During regular conferences they can then compare observations with the teacher more appropriately. In this way parents and teachers know what they are looking for, share in assessing the child all along, cooperate in efforts to help the child progress, and avoid

last minute confrontations, panics, and mutual reproaches. Rather, the repeated sharing of knowledge and
related feelings will have built a relationship of mutual
respect and trust between parents and teachers so that
they can together approach the last phase, namely preparing the child for kindergarten entry.

The school's preparatory activities and discussion will
help the children to the extent that their parents can
support this work and extend it into the home. Above all,
parents have to know that children are bound to have
mixed feelings about going to kindergarten and that it
helps them when parents listen sympathetically to their
concerns and misgivings. Some parents are afraid to listen for fear of what they will hear. Others who do listen
get so worried when they hear, "I don't want to go to
kindergarten," that they are tempted to preach or to ca-
jole or to persuade the child how nice it will be. It is
difficult for parents to believe that the child needs a true
friend who can ask calmly why the child does not want
to go to kindergarten, a friend who is willing to hear
about their worries, to talk them over, and to help the
child tolerate them. Sometimes the child's apprehensions
are warranted, sometimes not, but in either case it helps
when mother says, "Well, I guess it will be hard at times
but you'll make it. And if it's hard you can always tell
me about it after you come home. It's just important to
do a good job while you are there." A child views a new
school as an adult anticipates a new job. Would it not be
foolish to expect everything to be wonderful, and right
away at that? Indeed, I would be concerned that the child
who does not mention kindergarten or has only positive
things to say about it is not preparing himself adequately.

Another way that parents can help prepare children
is by actually taking the child to the school and helping
him to familiarize himself with all aspects of it as much

as possible. Visits to the kindergarten room and meetings with the teacher may have to be limited to a one-time experience, but getting to know the walk to and from school and the school yard can be repeated daily throughout the summer months till the child gradually feels confident that he can get there and back and can weather the real and imaginary hazards of walking to school and of spending recess in the playground. As mentioned earlier, nursery school teachers often arrange trial school bus rides for children who will use the bus. Mothers can help also by driving their child along the bus route to and from the school, perhaps even following a school bus, and by observing with the child the loading and unloading procedures in the school parking lot. Parents sometimes forget that their own knowledge of the school and neighborhood is not the child's, and that children do not get to know new things in one go but need many exposures and practice times. The long process of introducing the child to the concrete reality of his school-to-be also provides excellent opportunities for talking about his related feelings and coming to terms with them.

WHEN KINDERGARTEN READINESS HAS NOT BEEN ACHIEVED

All-out success is not the reward for our efforts. Even when we assess children's readiness potential early, help parents look for the right things, build a trusting relationship with them, and cooperate with them in helping the individual child to overcome lags or difficulties, there will still be some children who will not fulfill sufficiently the kindergarten readiness criteria. However, even with these youngsters we will have made some important gains to aid us in formulating our final recommendation and in sharing it with the parents in a helpful way. But what should that recommendation be?

It is a common mistake to think that an extra year in the nursery school will cure all ills—the child's troubles as well as the parents' and teacher's painful concerns. In my experience, the hope that another year will make troubles or lags disappear of their own accord invariably proves false.

The additional nursery school year works fruitfully only if one can be fairly sure that the difficulties one has pinpointed have a chance to be corrected by mother, teacher, and child working on them; if one has embarked on a plan of working on them; and if there has been some initial success to show that the problems indeed can be approached in this manner.

There is one other instance when an extra year in nursery school can be helpful, namely when the child is receiving professional psychiatric help with his difficulties and when that treatment program is furthered by, and coordinated with, the nursery school's work with the child and family. In this case the recommendation for additional nursery school experience does not come from the teacher or parents but from the psychiatrist or therapist. The latter then also outlines and supports the role of the nursery school in the joint approach to the problems.

Most children, however, are not helped by remaining in nursery school. On the contrary, not entering kindergarten at the appropriate developmental time can add to their difficulties. In terms of intellectual growth it is important to realize that the kindergartener experiences a maturational drive to learn and to work. If the child's educational environment does not provide adequate support and scope for this drive, it subsides and cannot be recaptured later. A child who starts academic learning and working when he is a year or two older does not necessarily catch on faster. He may actually learn more slowly and with less zest because he has missed out on utilizing the crest of the maturational learning drive and on developing basic working skills.

In a similar vein, it may be a mistake to hold back a child in order to spare him the hardships of kindergarten adjustment or to hope that it will be easy for him to get along in kindergarten when he is older than most of his peers. Personality strengths do not develop automatically when the child is ready but depend on practice in meeting challenges and overcoming frustrations and disappointments. We accept this as a matter of course in the area of physical growth, taking it for granted that muscles atrophy when not adequately exercised. We tend to forget the role of practice in developing mental strength. There is no way to enter kindergarten without experiencing hardship, which in turn develops skills for overcoming other hurdles. By contrast the child who is "spared" may miss out on this practice and command even less stamina later.

Further, we need to consider the lowering of self-esteem which usually attends not joining one's peers in kindergarten at the same age and being the oldest among them later on.

As far as the child's difficulties are concerned it is also important to keep in mind that the extra year without a carefully planned treatment program can allow problems to "lock in" so that they become more severe and less accessible to intervention.

What then can we recommend for the "not ready" child whose needs we cannot be sure of meeting in another year of nursery school? The answer is to ask for help: In practical terms this means effecting a referral for a psychiatric evaluation and recommendation.[1] This is easily said but is one of the most difficult tasks a teacher has to undertake. In some of our consultation groups with teachers we have worked on this topic at length and have published our experiences and suggestions (Goldsmith, 1971; Raia, 1975; Schiff, 1980). I shall not attempt to deal fully with the problems of referral here but restrict myself to highlighting some aspects of the issue.

The decision to take one's child to a psychiatrist or psychiatric agency represents a major injury to the parents' self-esteem and is most stressful for them. The suggestion for a referral therefore cannot be made unless and until teacher and parents have been able to build a mutually trusting relationship which has been tested in the joint talks about, and work on, the child's difficulties. When teacher and parent have looked at the child's problems together, have done their best to help him resolve them, and have recognized their own limitations, the way has been paved for the step of seeking outside help. The teacher's competent knowledge of the local resources is necessary and enables her often to build a helpful bridge to a specific professional in the field of mental health. But even the most skilled psychiatrist initially does not have a relationship with the parents. This further increases their stress and makes it essential for them to use the nursery school teacher throughout the lengthy evaluation process. The teacher has to be available for the parents to gather support, to overcome disappointments, to clarify misunderstandings, to listen to doubts and misgivings. This holds true even at that later point when the parents have to face a psychiatric assessment and follow through on a recommendation. Without the

[1] This differs from a psychological test whose main function is to determine the child's intellectual potential and achievements.

teacher's tactful ongoing assistance a successful referral can never be accomplished; even with it there are sometimes failures.

Last but not least, let us not forget the feelings of the child who has the difficulties and our need for his cooperation when we wish to help him or have others help him. We have talked of the need to be honest with the parents in helping them to see the child's trouble areas early, in enlisting their efforts to help resolve them, and in accepting additional professional help when necessary. In the same way, the teacher and the parents have to assist the child all along in seeing his own shortcomings, in trying to overcome them, and in utilizing the help we or others can offer him. This requires much understanding, tact, and respect for the child, an appreciation of his feelings, and an ability to help him recognize and tolerate them. It is impossible to help anyone with problems against their will or without their knowledge. Even the most loving parents, most devoted teacher, and most skilled psychiatrist can help a child only when he wants to master his difficulties and views the adults as helpers in this task.

Prevention, of course, is always easier than cure. Early recognition of developmental lags and interferences and concerted teacher–parent–child cooperation to work on them throughout the nursery school years often help to forestall the need for later therapeutic intervention. This is a difficult, yet important task for teachers to keep in mind. We are often so glad when we finally manage to assist a child in adjusting to the nursery school setting that it is hard for us to appreciate that the next developmental step, preparation for kindergarten, should already be under way.

Afterword

In discussing selected topics we have not attempted to provide simple answers to complex questions, but to share our way of working with some common preschool concerns, of learning to understand them, and of developing approaches which have proved helpful to young children and their families.

Preschoolers bring special pleasures and satisfactions to all of us who, in whatever capacity, work with or care for them. They also confront us daily with the most difficult and challenging aspects of education. They puzzle and frustrate us with their naughtiness and impulsiveness, with their lack of social graces and of inner restraints, and with their many idiosyncracies which so often seem impervious to logic or reason. These inevitable predicaments are no doubt one reason why teachers, parents, and mental health professionals look to each other for help and support, and why we want to work together to try and deepen our understanding, share our experiences, and learn from one another. A second, perhaps more important reason is our shared sense of bearing a special responsibility. The preschool age is a most crucial and vulnerable developmental level during which much of the foundation of later personality growth is laid. Preventive measures are especially effective at that time. This offers us unique opportunities to assist youngsters with developmental tasks and to further their chances for future emotional health. We want to extend our knowledge and perfect our skills in order to utilize these special educational opportunities to our charges' best advantage, to contribute our share, to touch their lives in a helpful way.

Erna Furman

References

Barnes, M. J. (1964), Reactions to the death of a mother. *Psychoanalytic Study of the Child*, 19: 334–357. New York: International Universities Press.

Freud, A. (1963), The concept of developmental lines. *Psychoanalytic Study of the Child*, 18: 245–265. New York: International Universities Press.

Furman, E. (1969a), Observations on entry to nursery school. *Bull. Philadelphia Assn. Psychoanal.*, 19(3): 133–152.

—————— (1969b), Schema of lines of development and mastery of tasks. In: *The Therapeutic Nursery School*, ed. R. A. Furman & A. Katan. New York: International Universities Press, pp. 298–309.

—————— (1974), *A Child's Parent Dies*. New Haven, CT: Yale University Press.

—————— (1980), Early latency—Normal and pathological aspects. In: *The Course of Life: Psychoanalytic Contributions Toward Understanding Personality Development*, ed. S. I. Greenspan & G. H. Pollock, Vol. II. *Latency, Adolescence and Youth*, Washington, D.C.: NIMH, U.S. Department of Health and Human Services, pp. 1–32.

—————— (1981), The high school course in child development. *Parent Education Newsletter of the Family Health Assn. of Cleveland*, 9(1): 1, 4.

—————— (1982), Mothers have to be there to be left. *Psychoanalytic Study of the Child*, 37: 15–28. New Haven, CT: Yale University Press.

Furman, R. A. (1964), Death of a six-year-old's mother during his analysis. *Psychoanalytic Study of the Child*, 19: 377–397. New York: International Universities Press.

—————— (1968), Excerpts from the analysis of a child with a congenital defect. *Internat. J. Psycho-Anal.*, 49: 276–279.

—————— Katan, A. (1969), *The Therapeutic Nursery School*. New York: International Universities Press.

Goldsmith, L. (1971), The referral process: Where do we start? *CAEYC*

Review, Fall: 7–11. Cleveland: Cleveland Association for the Education of Young Children.

Hoffman, Y. (1974), Learning about death in preschool. *CAEYC Review*, Spring: 15–17. Cleveland: Cleveland Association for the Education of Young Children.

Katan, A. (1961), Some thoughts about the role of verbalization in early childhood. *Psychoanalytic Study of the Child*, 16: 184–188. New York: International Universities Press.

Kirst, L. (1976), Anger—Telling it like it is. *CAEYC Review*, Spring: 7–11. Cleveland: Cleveland Association for the Education of Young Children.

Klaus, M.H., & Kennell, J. H. (1976), *Maternal and Infant Bonding*. St. Louis: C. V. Mosby Co.

McDonald, M. (1963), Helping children to understand death: An experience with death in a nursery school. *J. Nursery Ed.*, 19(1): 19–25.

Raia, L. (1975), A teacher's role in guiding parents toward a referral. *CAEYC Review*, Spring: 10–16. Cleveland: Cleveland Association for the Education of Young Children.

Sabath, N., Eber, C., Hoffman, Y., & Wagner, A. (1981), Guideline for child observation evaluation. *CAEYC Review*, Fall: 18–28. Cleveland: Cleveland Association for the Education of Young Children.

Schiff, E. (1980), What failures in referral have taught us. *CAEYC Review*, Spring: 27–30. Cleveland: Cleveland Association for the Education of Young Children.

Steininger, V., & Krueger, R. (1971), Kindergarten readiness: Looking beyond. *CAEYC Review*, Spring: 8–12. Cleveland: Cleveland Association for the Education of Young Children.

Winnicott, D. W. (1940), Communication at the scientific meeting of the British Psychoanalytic Society. Reported in M. Khan, J. A. Davis, & M. E. V. Davis (1974), The beginnings and fruition of the self—An essay on D. W. Winnicott. In: *Scientific Foundations of Paediatrics*, ed. J. A. Davis & J. Dobbing. London: W. B. Saunders Co., pp. 625–641.

——— (1964), *The Child, the Family and the Outside World*. New York: Penguin Books.

Index